Quilter's Bounty

Extraordinary Quilts
from Ordinary Blocks

Robin Strobel

Martingale ®
& COMPANY

Quilter's Bounty: Extraordinary Quilts from
Ordinary Blocks
© 2004 by Robin Strobel

That Patchwork Place® is an imprint of
Martingale & Company®.

Martingale & Company
20205 144th Avenue NE
Woodinville, WA 98072-8478 USA
www.martingale-pub.com

Printed in China
09 08 07 06 05 04   8 7 6 5 4 3 2 1

Library of Congress Cataloging-in-Publication Data

Strobel, Robin.
    Quilter's bounty : extraordinary quilts from
ordinary blocks / Robin Strobel.
        p. cm.
    Includes bibliographical references.
    ISBN 1-56477-527-5
    1. Patchwork—Patterns. 2. Quilting. I. Title.
    TT835.S74524 2004
    746.46'041—dc22
                                              2004010493

Mission Statement

Dedicated to providing quality products
and service to inspire creativity.

Credits

President: Nancy J. Martin

CEO: Daniel J. Martin

Publisher: Jane Hamada

Editorial Director: Mary V. Green

Managing Editor: Tina Cook

Technical Editor: Cyndi Hershey

Copy Editor: Melissa Bryan

Design Director: Stan Green

Illustrator: Laurel Strand

Cover and Text Designer: Regina Girard

Photographer: Brent Kane

Acknowledgments

I was raised in a family that values independence, and not until I faced some of life's battles did I realize that in many circumstances, receiving help is nothing to be ashamed of. In fact, the experiences that result from accepting other people's assistance are often more valuable than if I were doing everything on my own. Many of the quilts shown on these pages were made by friends who offered to help me turn this book into a reality. These generous quilters brought a depth of experience and skill (and fabric stashes) to this book far beyond that of which I was capable. Still other friends helped me bind quilts, understood when I holed up for days on end, and provided technical support when my computer went haywire. (Yes, Myles, I will vacuum the crumbs and cat hair out of the keyboard. Soon. I promise.)

So, thank you Laurel, Regina, Karen, and Terry, and also Janice, Shelley, and Margy. Your quilts are terrific. Thanks also to Pam Clarke in Spokane, Washington, who quilted 10 of the quilts, and to Janice Nelson in Kent, Washington, who quilted the other 4. Your skills and creativity exceed mine. Lynn and Ken Serack are two of the kindest friends anyone could wish for. A special "bless you" to Trish Carey, who encourages, listens, supports . . . and binds!

Contents

In Search of Quilted Treasures

Quilt blocks are beautiful in and of themselves, but I always experience a special thrill when I set blocks together, step back, and see the combined rows forming large sweeping patterns across the quilt top. Secondary patterns, invisible when you're looking at a solitary block, can add the illusion of depth and movement across a quilt's surface. I always feel like I'm uncovering buried treasure when I create this type of quilt. Anticipation is balanced by uncertainty. Have I understood the instructions? Will I uncover my treasure, or have I moved in the wrong direction and muddled the pattern? Sometimes the treasure I find is even richer than I had dreamed, and the quilt surpasses my expectations.

This book focuses on single blocks that, when set next to themselves, form beautiful, dynamic secondary designs. Quilting history is filled with traditional patterns of this type. I am including some of my favorites, such as Snail's Trail, Jacob's Ladder, Kaleidoscope, and Road to Oklahoma. I also offer patterns for lesser-known blocks and variations. Look at "Butterfly Garden" on page 44 and "Double Star" on page 78 for some interesting twists on tradition.

One of the biggest challenges for many quilters is choosing fabrics. I know that by the time you read this book, many of the fabrics shown will be unavailable. So, at the beginning of each project, I am including a section on successful fabric selection. Hopefully, this will help take some of the uncertainty out of creating your own spectacular quilts. Choose

any pattern in this book, follow the instructions and hints, and discover your own quilted treasures.

The quilts are fairly simple and easy to construct. Often several different techniques can be used to make the blocks or the smaller units within the blocks. In the following section, "Quilting Basics," I explain the methods I find useful. I urge you to try new techniques and use the ones that you find most satisfying. Sometimes I prefer strip piecing, while at other times I find just cutting out the individual shapes and sewing them together is easier. If accuracy and sharp little points are of paramount importance, I may turn to foundation paper piecing. We all have different skills and abilities, likes and dislikes. A technique that is perfect for one person may be a nightmare for another. Learn what works for you and you will increase your quilting enjoyment!

Now I offer a word to the perfectionist that lives in us all. The quilts in this book contain triangles. Triangles have points that, in a perfect world, would end exactly at a seam. If you plan on entering a quilt in a national, juried show, let your perfectionist self run crazy—the judges and viewers are going to stick their noses right in the fabric to make certain each pesky little point ends exactly where it should. But face it: Most of the quilts we make are for our family, our friends, or ourselves. You want to make beautiful quilts, and you want to make them well, but every point and seam in every quilt you make does not have to be perfect. Consider who is going to receive the quilt and how it will be used. Is it for a non-quilting friend with a new baby, for a young child, or for someone who is ill? None of these people will care what your triangles look like. They will love the colors and designs and the fact that you took the time to make something for them. It is more important for you simply to make these quilts, enjoy the process, and get them completed than it is to fuss, rip, and resew recalcitrant points. Before you rip out a seam, ask yourself, "Can I live with it?" If you can, just keep going! The only thing you have to promise yourself is that you will not, for any reason, point out this imperfection to anyone else!

Quilting Basics

Quilting is supposed to be fun, creative, and rewarding. As with most things creative, there are inevitably times of frustration, disappointment, and confusion. If you find yourself in a quilting quandary, or if my project instructions don't make sense, you may wish to read through this section. The truth of the matter is there are usually three or four different methods that will all achieve good results. I offer to you a condensed version of the quilting techniques that I find most useful, with full appreciation that you may find a different way of doing things that works better for you.

Must Have Fabric!

Many quilters have a love/hate relationship with fabric. They love fabrics—the colors, the textures, and the patterns—but hate choosing fabrics for their quilts. I admit to the part about loving fabric. Recently, my stash grew too heavy for the shelves, and the entire unit came crashing down on me! As an avalanche of fabric knocked me to the floor, I imagined the headline in the local paper: "Woman Killed by Falling Fabric." (I wasn't hurt, but I did march out and buy the super-strong shelving units that will hold 1,500 pounds apiece!)

For each of the patterns in this book, I thought long and hard about what fabric choices would contribute to the designs. Striking secondary patterns are created through contrast. We can create contrast through color, value, and different visual textures (the type and size of a print). Of these three, value (how light or dark each fabric appears against another) is perhaps the most critical to a design. To make things even more interesting, the value of a specific fabric is relative; it depends on the other surrounding fabrics.

The same fabric looks dark in value when compared to the first two fabrics and light when compared to the second two fabrics.

Sometimes the light or dark value of a fabric is difficult to predict. Some fabrics contain wide value shifts within themselves. Batiks as well as large-scale prints may be light in one section and dark in another. Consider how large or small the pieces will be that you are planning to cut from a fabric. Make a frame roughly that size with your fingers. Move your fingers over different sections of the fabric.

7

Does the value shift dramatically? If so, you won't want to use that print in a value-critical position in your quilt.

This batik and large-scale print both contain dramatic shifts in value.

I am often fooled by prints that have a dark background with a medium-sized, lighter-value pattern. I know the background will still be seen when the fabric is cut into small pieces, so I tend to think that the fabric is fairly dark in value. What I fail to take into account is that the background becomes less dominant, although still visible, after the fabric is cut, and the small pieces actually look lighter than I thought they would be. I will confess, I made this mistake with one quilt in this book. After I'd pieced the entire quilt top, I found I could not live with the value of that print. I thought, and huffed, and whined, and slept on it. I realized that while the quilt was pretty, and in normal circumstances I would have been happy with it, I felt the secondary design was not strong enough for the quilt to work well for this book. However, I also did not want to re-create the entire quilt! So, I did what any self-respecting "casual quilter" would do. I very carefully and delicately shaded in each and every piece of that fabric in my quilt top using a

Compare the values of your fabric choices. A wide range in value will create strong, vivid patterns, as in the blue-and-white quilt above. A closer range in value will create softer patterns, as in the blue-and-yellow quilt. If your fabrics have no difference in value, the pattern on your quilt will hardly be noticeable.

permanent fabric marking pen! Normally, I would never tell anyone I did this, but I think you should know that every quilter makes mistakes, and the solutions to those mistakes may be unconventional.

These are the types of fabrics that fool me into thinking they are darker than they really are.

When I consider color for a quilt, I usually don't worry about selecting fabric according to a predetermined color scheme. (There are exceptions, such as my strict adherence to blue and yellow in "Spring Fling" on page 38.) Instead, I think of a general "look" that I want for my quilt and then roam the fabric stores in search of fabrics that suit my mood. I may be looking for bright, vibrant children's prints, or soft country colors, or maybe something elegant and serene. I have a general idea of the value range I'm looking for, but not the specific color. Usually, there will be a print that captures my attention. Using that print as a guide, I'll select the other fabrics for the quilt.

I want to find fabrics that enhance this first print while contrasting effectively with it as well. In addition to value, different visual textures can create contrast. If my first fabric is a medium-scale print, I often look for subtle tone-on-tone prints that share a similar color with the first. I prefer tone-on-tone prints to solids because they add a visual richness I find

pleasing. The colors do not need to match perfectly—a little variety can add a bit of sparkle to the quilt.

Subtle tone-on-tone prints contrast nicely with a medium-scale multicolor fabric.

Cutting

Accuracy starts here. You can sew perfect ¼" seams, but if you don't cut accurately, you will have a never-ending struggle to get your pieces to fit. I am incapable of accuracy using the lines on a cutting mat, so I use two rulers to achieve a precise cut. I use a 6" x 24" ruler to cut against and a second ruler for measuring. You can use almost any size of ruler for measuring, but most quilters have a 6" x 12" ruler, which works well.

1. Iron all of the fabrics that will be used in the quilt. Fold each one, wrong sides together, with opposite selvage edges aligned. If the fabric has been cut off-grain, shift the selvage edges in opposite directions until the wrinkles disappear. Lay the fabric on the rotary-cutting mat with the folded edge toward you.

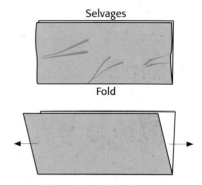

Selvages

Fold

Shift until wrinkles disappear.

TIP It is annoying when your ruler tilts sideways as you cut against it, so I use an inchworm approach to cutting. I start with my hand near the base of the ruler and cut to a height just above my fingertips. Then, without moving the cutter or ruler, I bring the thumb of the hand bracing the ruler up to just below my fingers and extend my fingers to brace the top half of the ruler. I then cut the remainder of the strip. I also use a clear plastic film (available at most quilt stores) on the wrong side of the ruler to help keep it from slipping.

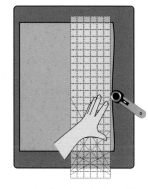

Pause cutting level with tips of fingers
but do not lift cutter from fabric.

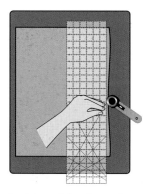

"Inchworm" hand up ruler.

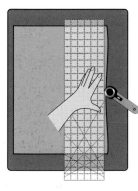

Continue cutting.

2. If cutting strips of identical width from several fabrics, layer them, slightly offsetting the folded edges. Depending on your skill level and the sharpness of your rotary cutter, you can layer up to six fabrics and still make perfect cuts.

3. Straighten one end of the fabric by aligning a horizontal line on the 6" x 24" ruler with the folded edge of the fabric. Position the ruler only as far in from the raw edges as needed to cut through all layers of fabric. Cut along the long edge of the ruler. Be certain all layers have a clean, straight edge.

4. Use a second ruler to measure a strip of the appropriate width from the straightened edge. Place the 6" x 24" (cutting) ruler against the edge of the measuring ruler. If your measuring ruler is shorter than the width of the folded fabric, slide it up and down the 6" x 24" ruler to be certain the strip you cut measures the same at every point. Set the measuring ruler aside and cut along the 6" x 24" ruler's edge.

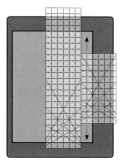

Slide measuring ruler
to check accuracy.

5. Every three or four strips, check to be certain the strips are perpendicular to the fold of the fabric. If not, follow step 3 to straighten the edge.

I use this same two-ruler method for cutting squares and rectangles from the strips, and for cutting segments from strip sets. If cutting squares or rectangles, use the edge of the strip to align the ruler when you make your cleanup cut. If cutting strip sets, align the ruler with one of the seams.

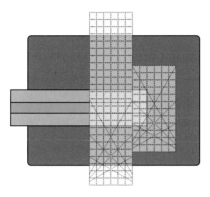

Some of the quilts in this book require you to use a template to cut a triangle shape. Trace the pattern onto a piece of template plastic, which is available either at your quilt store or through mail order. Using an old blade in your rotary cutter, place the edge of a ruler along one of the long drawn lines and cut the plastic directly on the line. Repeat with the other edges of the pattern. Set the ruler aside and use the rotary cutter to trim the tips on any triangle points, if needed. Place the template back over the pattern in the book and check to make certain you have cut it accurately. Place the template on the strip of fabric as directed in the instructions. Align the short edge of the template with one of the long edges of the fabric strip. Place a ruler along the edge of the template and hold it in position. Set the template aside and, with a sharp blade in your rotary cutter, cut along the edge of the ruler. Put the template back on the fabric strip just as before, but match both the short side and the cut side edge. Place the ruler along the long uncut edge of the template. Set the template aside and cut along the edge of the ruler. If the template has trimmed triangle tips, you can trim them from the fabric piece at this time. Once you have cut

your first piece, rotate the template 180°, and place it back on the fabric strip. This time the short edge of the template will be on the opposite edge of the fabric strip from its placement during the first cut. Cut your second piece as you did the first. While it is easier to just cut alongside the edge of the template instead of using a ruler, template plastic slices easily and slivers can get shaved off, causing the template to be inaccurate.

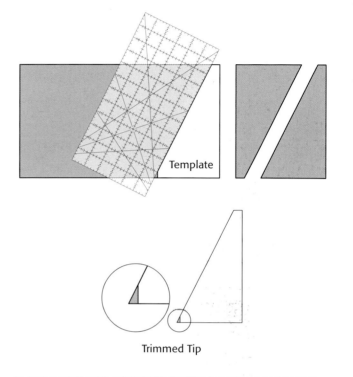

Trimmed Tip

> **TIP** Mark the right side of the template so that you know which side to keep facing you when cutting. Some of the patterns in this book require the triangles to be cut with the diagonal slanting in a specific direction. If you flip the template, you will end up cutting the triangles incorrectly.

Piecing Triangles

Quilters have developed several timesaving methods for creating different units that contain triangles. Most of the triangles used in this book are called half-square triangles, because the shape is that of a square that has been cut in half on the diagonal.

Notice that the long edge of this type of triangle is cut on the bias, and, as a result, it stretches easily.

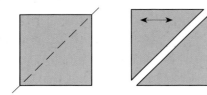

Two half-square triangles are often sewn together to make a half-square-triangle unit, also called a triangle square. I know of at least five different techniques for sewing these shapes. Perhaps the most popular method is to create two such units at a time. To do so, cut a square of each fabric ⅞" larger than the desired finished size of the half-square-triangle unit. Mark a diagonal line from corner to corner on the wrong side of the lighter fabric square. Place the two fabric squares right sides together, and stitch ¼" on either side of the marked line. Accuracy is important here, so measure the seams on the first several units to be certain you are sewing ¼" from the line. Cut on the marked line and press each half-square-triangle unit toward the darker fabric.

Half-Square-
Triangle Unit

My favorite method is to make eight identical half-square-triangle units at a time. I have no idea who the brilliant quilter was who first thought of it, but my thanks go out to her! To make eight identical half-square-triangle units, take the desired finished size of the half-square-triangle unit and double it. Add 1¾" to this number, and cut a square of each fabric to this measurement. For example, if the finished size of the half-square-triangle unit is 2½", multiply this number by 2 (2½" x 2 = 5"). Now add 1¾" to 5" (1¾" + 5" = 6¾"). You will cut the squares 6¾". After the squares are cut, mark an X from

corner to corner on the wrong side of the lighter fabric square. Pin the squares right sides together and stitch ¼" on either side of the marked lines.

Place the stitched unit on your cutting mat, and position a ruler vertically so that the cutting edge runs directly through the middle of the squares. Carefully cut the square in half vertically and then horizontally. It is important that these two cuts be accurate. Now, cut the four pieces of the square along the drawn lines. (These cuts do not need to be particularly accurate.) Press each piece toward the darker fabric, and—like magic—you have eight half-square-triangle units.

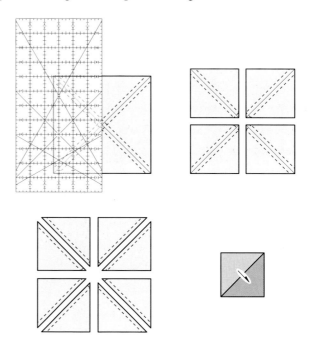

> **TIP** To find the center of the large square, add ⅞" to the desired finished measurement of the half-square-triangle unit, and that is where the middle of the square is located. In the preceding example, the center of the large square is 3⅜" from the raw edges (2½" + ⅞" = 3⅜"). While the math in the previous sentence explains the logic, a quicker way to achieve the same result is to simply divide the large square in half (6¾" ÷ 2 = 3⅜").

Half-square triangles may be added to other shapes; you might add them to a rectangle to create what is commonly called a "flying-geese" unit, or to the four corners of a square to make a "square-in-a-square" unit. Instead of using half-square triangles, I use what may be called the "folded-corner" technique to make these shapes. In each case, cut the fabric you are using for the smaller triangles into squares that are ½" larger than the finished side (short edge) of those triangles. Mark a diagonal line from corner to corner on the wrong side of each square. Place a square on top of the larger piece of fabric, right sides together, with the diagonal line positioned correctly to allow for trimming the corners. Stitch along the line. Fold the small square toward the corner to be certain it is sewn correctly, and then press it toward the corner. You will need to trim the excess fabric, leaving an approximate ¼" seam allowance. Most quilters like to trim the excess from both the small square and the larger shape. I usually trim the excess fabric from only the smaller square. The extra layer of fabric is hardly noticeable unless you hand quilt, and the resulting shape is both stable and an accurate size. When I work with a heavy, thick fabric such as flannel, I always trim both excess layers.

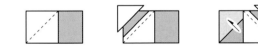

Flying-Geese Unit

Square-in-a-Square

■ General Piecing

Here are my tips for making the piecing process as easy and painless as possible.

Quilts pieced with triangles are much easier to sew together if you try to keep an accurate ¼" seam allowance. Even if you use a ¼" presser foot, you may find that your seams are slightly wider or narrower than a true ¼". I check my seam accuracy when I first start sewing a new project. Having said that, I admit that after the first units are sewn, I pay less attention to the correct seam width and focus more on getting the pieces together with seams aligned and the tips of the triangles tidy at the seams.

My sewing machine tends to swallow the beginning strands of thread, tangle them up, and form a large knot under the bottom piece of fabric. To keep this from occurring, I start and stop on a small scrap of fabric.

When possible, I take an assembly-line approach to sewing, feeding pieces through the machine one after the other and stopping to cut the thread only when an entire group is sewn. This is called chain piecing.

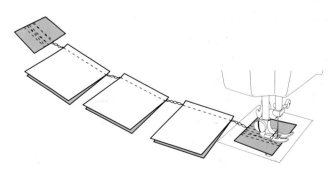

I seldom pin individual pieces together before sewing, and I also do not pin units together unless I need to match a triangle point. I make certain that the seam allowances that are supposed to match are pressed in opposite directions and then use my fingers to pinch and regulate the fabric as I feed it under the presser foot. About half of my students like this technique, while the other half are more successful when they pin. Use the technique that gives you the best results. If you pin, you can help avoid damage to your machine if you remove the pins just before crossing over them with your needle.

Opposing Seams

Sometimes, when one portion of the seam allowance has already been stitched down, such as when you are stitching blocks into rows, you will find that opposing seams might be pressed in the *same* direction, making them difficult to align accurately. My solution to this problem is to finger-press one seam in the opposite direction before sewing. The disadvantage to this technique is that it causes a twist in the seam allowance, which can form a tiny lump on the front of the quilt. The lump usually disappears, but some people like to cut a ⅛" notch in the seam where the twist occurs.

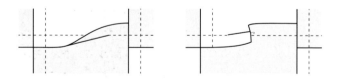

For the first four years that I made quilts, I avoided any patterns containing triangles. Triangles terrified me, and my first few experiences with them were, literally, not pretty. Over the years, I've learned how to get the points of the triangles to match. It may not be precision quilting, but it works for me.

First, I try to sew an extremely accurate ¼" seam on the initial seams of the triangle. After that, I don't worry too much about the width of the seam allowance on the part of the block that contains the triangle point. I just sew the seam allowance to accommodate the point of the triangle. Any wobble in the seam can usually be pressed or quilted out and is not noticeable. The point of the triangle, which *is* very visible, will look sharp and accurate.

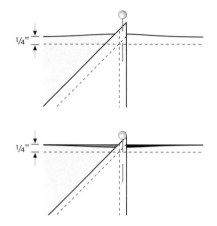

If possible, I sew with the triangle on top so that I can easily see the point. Pin through the seams, making certain that any opposing seams match. Stitch, aiming for one thread-width beyond the triangle point. Remove the pin just before sewing over it. When the fabric is opened and pressed, the point will appear to be perfect.

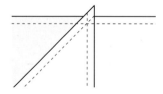

Sewing with the triangle on top is not always possible. Try this technique if the triangle is on the bottom layer. Pin the fabrics together, making certain that opposing seams match. Stab a pin straight through the tip of the triangle point through the top layer. Make a mark on the top layer directly where the pin exits the fabric. Stitch directly through the marked point.

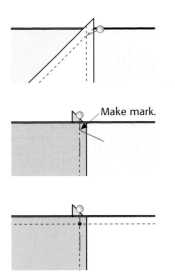

Make mark.

No matter how often I sew triangles, sometimes I miss sewing accurate points. When I miss, first I ask myself how bad it looks and if I can live with it. If it does not look too bad, and/or if I can live with it, I leave it. If I decide I want to fix it, I correct only the small area that bothers me.

There are two basic fixes. If the opposing seams match but the seam allowance is too narrow, this allows a gap between the point and the seam. If this is the case, I simply restitch, taking a larger bite. Sew with the triangle on top, even if you originally stitched with the triangle on the bottom.

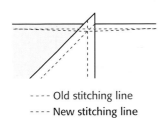

- - - - Old stitching line
- - - - New stitching line

If the seam allowance is too wide (cutting off the point), and/or the seams do not match, I take out the original stitching, usually up to the last place at which a seam or point matched correctly. I pin the point and a few places in between. Start by over-lapping the original stitching for five or six stitches, and then sew the section, easing and stretching as

needed to get the seams and points to match. (Remove the pins just before you sew over them.) End by sewing over the original stitching for five or six stitches.

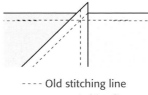

- - - - Old stitching line
- - - - New stitching line

If I still can't get the blasted point to match, I will finger-press the seams open, pin while matching the seams, and try stitching it that way. Sometimes this method works better for me than the opposing seams method. Use whatever approach you find to be most accurate. Pressing the seams open goes against conventional quilting wisdom, and people who quilt by hand probably will prefer to press their seams to one side.

I like to use the technique that will give me the best visual results. I don't care if it is called pressing or ironing, the idea is to get the fabric to lie flat without stretching it out of shape. I have a great history of creating many interesting shapes by stretching the fabric when I iron it. I iron more accurately without steam, but most people prefer steam. Be careful not to press pleats along the seam lines as you iron. If I press pleats into a seam allowance, or if I need to re-press for any reason, I spray a little water on the piece, fluff it, fold it back into the shape it had before pressing, and iron it flat so that it looks just like it did when I first sewed it. I then open the pieces and press them correctly.

Borders

You do not need to border your quilt if you do not want to. If you do want to add one or more borders, there are many variations possible. A border may be made from several fabrics, and each side may be a different width. Some of the quilts in this book have pieced borders that actually continue part of the block patterns. I usually do not decide on the number, size, and fabrics for borders until after I complete the center of the quilt. If one of my original fabrics does not look good as a border, I take the top to the quilt shop and audition different fabrics against it.

By the time a quilt's center is complete, it may not be a perfect rectangle or square. I use borders to help square a lopsided quilt.

1. Measure the length of the quilt top through the center. Cut two side border strips to this measurement. (If the borders are longer than 40", you will need more than one strip to make a border. In this case, I sew all the border strips together end to end, creating one long strip. I fold this strip in half, crosswise, and cut two borders at a time to the correct measurement.) Mark the midpoints of the border strips and the quilt top.

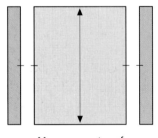

Measure center of quilt, top to bottom.

2. With right sides together, and raw ends and midpoints matching, sew the border strips to the sides of the quilt top, easing as necessary. Press the seam allowances toward the border strips.

Match ends and midpoints.

3. Measure the width of the quilt top through the center, including the side borders you just added. Cut two border strips to this measurement. Mark the midpoints of the border strips and quilt top. With right sides together, and raw ends and midpoints matching, sew the border strips to the top and bottom of the quilt top, easing as necessary. Press the seam allowances toward the border strips.

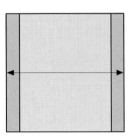 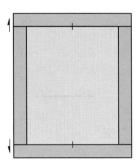

Measure center of quilt, left to right.

Match ends and midpoints.

Finishing

I love to machine quilt, am abysmal at hand quilting, and usually have time for neither. Fortunately, there are terrific machine quilters out there who will quilt my quilts for me. All of the quilts in this book were quilted by professionals who used long-arm quilting machines. Pam Clarke, from Spokane, Washington, quilted 10 of the quilts, and Janice Nelson, from Kent, Washington, quilted the other 4. Both ladies are extremely creative and skilled at quilting, and their designs do much to enhance the quilts.

If you decide to send your quilt to a professional machine quilter, ask your quilting friends whom they recommend. Ask the quilter how long her turnaround time is and how she structures her fees. Some quilters charge by the hour, and others charge by the square inch. There may be extra charges for using decorative threads, changing threads frequently, batting, shipping, and trimming. If possible, look at some of the quilts she has quilted and check the backs for even thread tension, knots, and tangled threads. Discuss with her what kinds of quilting you like and dislike and what types of designs and threads you want on your quilt. Remember, once you send your quilt away, what happens to it is out of your control. The quilt may come back more beautiful than you anticipated, but sometimes you might be disappointed. Once a quilt is machine quilted, it is extremely difficult to take out the quilting without damaging the fabric, so you will have to live with the results. Be prepared to pay for high-quality quilting.

If you decide to do your own quilting, whether by hand or machine, and you have never quilted before, I strongly advise taking a class or finding a mentor to help you through the tricky spots. There are also wonderful books that can be invaluable guides to machine-quilting and hand-quilting techniques. (See "Resources" on page 96.) Quilting is a skill that takes

some practice. I recommend starting on a small project rather than a king-size bedspread meant for your parents' 50th wedding anniversary. (I speak directly from experience on this!)

Whether you quilt the project yourself or send it out, you will need to make a back for the quilt. Most long-arm machine quilters will want you to give them a back that is about 6" larger than the quilt top. The project instructions for each quilt in this book specify the number of fabric widths needed and the placement of the seams used to piece them together. If you quilt it yourself, you can make the back just 4" larger. If you have confidence in the quilting, make the back out of a fabric that will highlight the stitching. If you are unsure you will like the quilting, a busy print will help hide it!

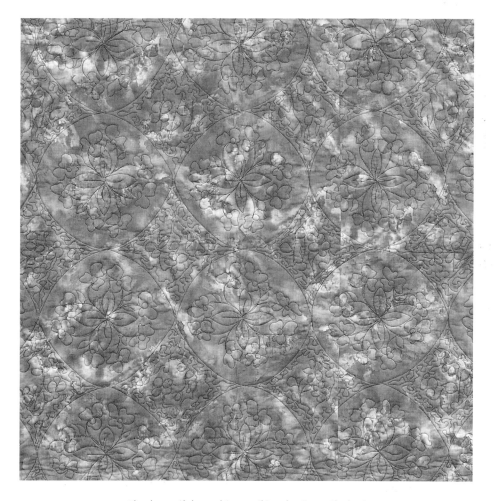

The beautiful machine quilting by Pam Clarke is clearly visible on the back of this quilt.

After the quilt is quilted, it is time to bind it. I usually use a French-fold binding cut on the straight of grain. If you make your quilt the same size as mine, the number of binding strips has been figured for you. If you make your quilt a different size, you will need to calculate how much binding you require.

1. Trim any excess batting and backing even with the edges of the quilt top. (Try to keep the borders even and the corners square.) Measure the length and width of your quilt. Add those numbers together, double it, and add 10". This is the total length you need to make your binding. For example, if your quilt measures 46½" x 58¼", you will need binding a total length of 219½". This was figured as follows:

   a. 46½" + 58¼" = 104¾"

   b. 104¾" x 2 = 209½"

   c. 209½" + 10" = 219½"

2. Divide the total length of binding by the width of your fabric to determine the number of strips you need to cut. Unfortunately, by the time the selvage is cut off, many quilters' fabrics are narrower than 42", so use 40" in your calculation just to be safe. You will need to round this number up to the next whole number, so in this example, six strips will need to be cut for the binding (219.5" ÷ 40" = 5.4875).

3. The width you cut your binding strips depends mostly on personal preference. The standard recommended width is 2½", and that is what I have used in the instructions. I prefer my binding a little thinner than most quilters, so I cut my binding strips 2¼" wide. Cut the number and size of binding strips needed for your quilt.

4. Join the binding strips end to end at a 45° angle to make one long binding strip. To do this, place two strips, right sides together, at right angles to each other and excluding the selvage edges. Sew as shown along the diagonal formed by the

junction of the two strips. Trim the seam to ¼" and press it open.

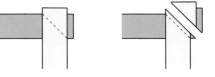

5. Trim the beginning end of the strip at a 45° angle and press under ¼". Fold the binding strip in half lengthwise, wrong sides together, and press.

Fold line

6. With the right side of the quilt facing up, align the raw edges of the binding strip with the raw edges of the quilt. If you have a walking foot for your machine using it can help feed the fabric evenly. Begin stitching about 3" past the beginning of the binding strip and not at a corner. Keep a "hefty" ¼" seam allowance, taking care that all the layers are flat and do not have any tucks or creases. Stitch to ¼" from the corner and stop with the needle down through the fabric.

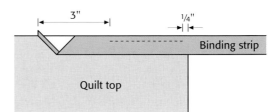

3"

¼"

Binding strip

Quilt top

7. Raise the presser foot and rotate the quilt 90°. Put the presser foot down and, reversing the stitching direction, stitch off the back edge of the quilt. Pull it slightly away from your sewing machine and fold the binding strip away from you and then back, as shown on the facing page. Keep the raw edges of both the binding and quilt even. Position the needle with a ¼" seam allowance from the side and stitch. Stitch

forward from the back edge, across the double layers of binding, maintaining your seam allowance. Continue sewing and turn the other three corners in the same manner.

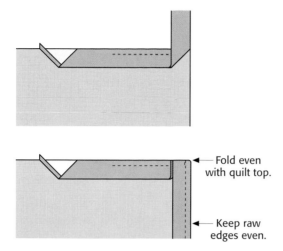

Fold even with quilt top.

Keep raw edges even.

8. You can join the beginning and end of the binding strip one of several ways. I prefer a simple method of trimming the end of the binding strip at a 45° angle with about ½" overlapping the beginning of the binding strip. (Be careful to make the cut in the same direction as the begin-

ning of the binding strip.) Tuck the end of the binding strip inside the beginning of the strip. Resume stitching along the raw edges, taking a few stitches past the start of the stitching. This technique can leave a little bump in the binding's edge, and you will have to whipstitch the overlapped edges by hand.

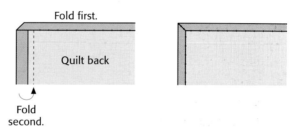

9. Fold the long, folded edge of the binding to the back of the quilt so that it just covers the stitching line and hand stitch the edge to the back. The corners will automatically form a miter when you stitch one side of the quilt first, and then fold the second side to the back.

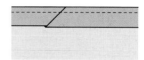

Fold first.

Quilt back

Fold second.

Pinwheels

Pieced by Margy Duncan. Quilted by Pam Clarke, 2003. Finished quilt size: 49½" x 63½". Finished block size: 7".

Dark and light pinwheels spin and overlap in this basic design. At first I hesitated to use the black fabric with a sparkly Mylar-type design because I was not certain it was sturdy enough. When I got home, I immediately tossed it in the washer and dryer and then tried pressing it with a moderately cool iron. I'm pleased to report that, so far, this fabric has been very well behaved. I love the extra sparkle and shifting glimmer of color it adds to the quilt.

Successful Fabric Selection

I wanted this quilt to be simple, vibrant, and dynamic, so I chose a black print for the background. I added bright, clear tone-on-tone colors from the same line of fabric (Color Tree from In The Beginning Fabrics). The key to the design is to keep a good contrast between the background and the other fabrics. This quilt offers a great opportunity to achieve different looks by experimenting with your fabric selections. When choosing fabrics, place each fabric beside your selected background fabric and squint at them. If the fabrics are clearly different from each other, there will be a nice contrast in the block. If the fabrics blur together, your quilt will look soft and unfocused, and the pattern will not be very distinct.

Materials

Yardage is based on 42"-wide fabric.

3 yards of black print for block background, border, and binding

Fat quarter each of 12 medium to light tone-on-tone prints in bright colors*

3 yards for backing (2 widths pieced horizontally)

53" x 68" piece of batting

*I actually used a bundle of fat-eighth pieces (9" x 20") and had barely enough fabric. Using fat eighths is a little risky because there is not much room for error.

Cutting

Note: Strips are cut across the width of the fabric unless indicated otherwise.

From each of the bright prints, cut:
2 squares, 8¾" x 8¾"

From the black print, cut:
6 strips, 8¾" x 42"; crosscut into 24 squares, 8¾" x 8¾"
6 strips, 4" x 42"
6 strips, 2½" x 42"

Assembly

Each block is made using the following unit:

4 Half-Square-
Triangle Units

1. To make the half-square-triangle units, mark an X from corner to corner on the wrong side of a bright square. Layer this square with a black square, right sides together. Sew ¼" on each side of the marked lines. Cut the squares first vertically and then horizontally through the center (4⅜" from the edges). Be careful to make accurate cuts. Cut each piece diagonally on the marked lines and press seams toward the dark

21

fabric. Repeat with the remaining squares to make 16 half-square-triangle units from each bright tone-on-tone fabric.

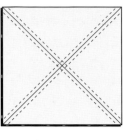

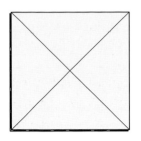

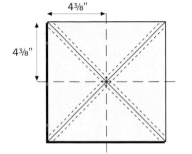

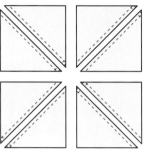

Make 16
of each color.

2. Arrange four matching half-square-triangle units as shown. Sew into rows and press toward the dark triangles. Sew the rows together. Press the seams open, or in one direction. Make four Pinwheel blocks from each bright color.

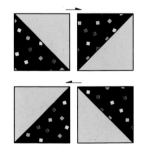

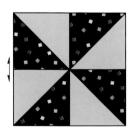

Make 4 of each color
(48 total).

3. Arrange the blocks in eight rows of six blocks each. You can fuss with the color arrangement as much or as little as you like. I get much the same result whether I spend an hour or a week arranging the blocks; plus, after I sew the top together there are inevitably at least two or three blocks I want to reposition! Sew the blocks into rows and press in alternate directions from row to row. Sew the rows together. Press.

4. Sew the 4" border strips together end to end to make one long strip. Measure the length of the quilt top through the center and cut two border strips to this size. Sew the strips to the sides of the quilt top. Press toward the borders. Measure the width of the quilt top through the center and cut two border strips to this size. Sew to the

top and bottom of the quilt. Press toward the borders.

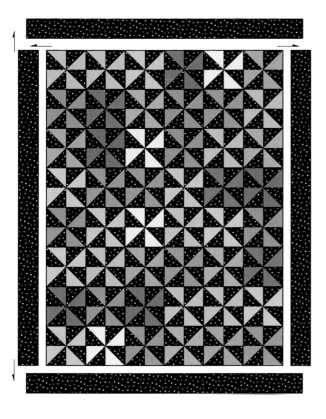

5. Layer the pieced backing, batting, and quilt top. Baste the layers together. I had fat-eighth pieces left over from the packet of fabrics I bought for the quilt top, so I sewed them together to make a pretty and colorful back.

6. Quilt as desired.

7. Prepare the binding and sew it to the quilt.

Alternative Fabric Selection

Margie Duncan, who pieced the quilt top for me, wants to make her own version of this pattern using rich floral fabrics. You could choose a fairly plain fabric for the background and a selection of floral prints for the blocks, or you could find a floral print you really love for the background and make the blocks from coordinating colors and prints. Remember, less contrast between the background and the other fabrics will result in a softer, less graphic-looking quilt—which may be exactly what you want! I would also like to see this quilt made with a cream-colored background and 1930s-era reproduction prints substituted for my tone-on-tone fabrics. Each of these suggestions will result in a very different look for your quilt.

A light-value floral print background gives this pattern a softer, more romantic look.

Vivid Imaginings

Made by Janice Nelson, 2003.
Finished quilt size: 64½" x 74½". Finished block size: 10".

The Jewel Box block dates from the 1930s and goes by many other names, such as Railroad, Hourglass, and World's Fair. My friend Janice, who has a notable stash of fabric, chose a different bright, fun print with a black background for each block and then paired each print with a colorful tone-on-tone fabric. I love the look of the bright chains and hourglasses because they seem to dance across the quilt top.

 ## Successful Fabric Selection

Select 30 medium-scale multicolor prints that have black backgrounds and bright colors. Janice's quilt has print motifs of cats, dinosaurs, shoes, flowers, dots, stars, kids, and fish (just to name a few). For each of the secondary prints, choose a bright medium-value tone-on-tone fabric. This is your chance to "run amuck" around the color wheel and work with fabrics and colors that you don't normally use. I usually advise making the quilt top before choosing the borders, but to tell the truth, almost any bright striped fabric looks great with this pattern. There are always many terrific kids' prints available, but don't despair if you have trouble finding 30 black-background prints and 30 tone-on-tone fabrics. Find 15 of each and make two blocks with the same fabric combination instead of just one.

Materials

Yardage is based on 42"-wide fabric.

1½ yards of solid black for inner border, border corners, and binding

1 yard of bright stripe for outer border

Fat eighth (9" x 20") each of 30 bright prints with black backgrounds for blocks*

Fat eighth (9" x 20") each of 30 bright tone-on-tone prints for blocks*

4 yards for backing (2 widths pieced horizontally)

69" x 79" piece of batting

Fat eighths can be hard to find. If you have to buy quarter-yard pieces, cut the excess into squares or rectangles and sew them together for the back. Not only will you feel thrifty and clever, you will also have a terrific-looking back for your quilt.

Cutting

Note: Strips are cut across the width of the fabric unless indicated otherwise.

From each of the prints with black backgrounds, cut:
4 squares, 3" x 3"
1 square, 5⅞" x 5⅞"

From each of the bright tone-on-tone prints, cut:
4 squares, 3" x 3"
1 square, 5⅞" x 5⅞"

From the solid black, cut:
6 strips, 3" x 42"
4 squares, 7½" x 7½"
8 strips, 2½" x 42"

From the bright stripe, cut:
6 strips, 5" x 42"

Assembly

Each block is made using the following units:

2 Four-Patch Units   2 Half-Square-Triangle Units

1. To make the four-patch units, sew two 3" black background squares to two companion 3" tone-on-tone squares. Press toward the black. Sew the two identical units together into a four-patch as shown. Press the seam in either direction. Repeat with the remaining 3" squares, keeping the same black-background print and tone-on-tone fabrics together. Make two four-patch units from each fabric pair.

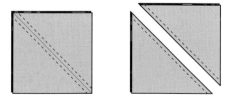

Make 2 of each
combination (60 total).

2. To make the half-square-triangle units, mark a diagonal line from corner to corner on the wrong side of each 5⅞" tone-on-tone square. Place each tone-on-tone square, right sides together, with a 5⅞" square of the same fabric it was paired with in the four-patch units. Stitch ¼" on each side of the marked line. Cut on the marked line and press toward the black-background fabric.

Make 2 of each
combination (60 total).

3. Arrange two four-patch units and two matching half-square-triangle units as shown. Be careful to position the units correctly. My favorite mistake is to rotate a unit 90° and not notice it until the top is all sewn together. Sew the units into rows and then join the rows. Press as shown. Make 30 blocks.

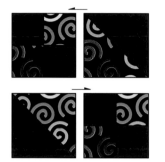 

Make 1 of each
combination (30 total).

4. Arrange the blocks into six rows of five blocks each, alternating the rotation of the blocks 90° as shown. You will see bright tone-on-tone four-patches and on-point squares where the blocks meet. Sew the blocks into rows. Press in alternate directions from row to row. Sew the rows together and press.

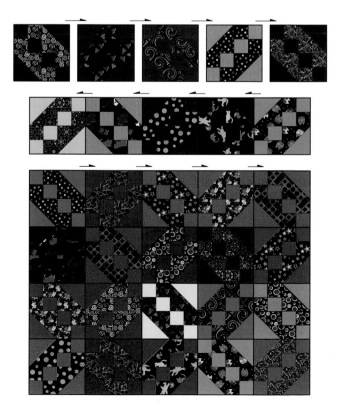

26

5. Sew the 3" inner-border strips together end to end to make one long strip. Sew the 5" outer-border strips together end to end to make another long strip. Sew the inner and outer border strips together along the long edges. Press toward the black. Measure the length of the quilt top through the center and cut two side border strips to this size. Measure the width of the quilt top through the center and cut a top border and a bottom border to this size. Sew a 7½" black square to each end of the top and bottom border strips. Press toward the strips. Sew the side border strips to the quilt top, and press toward the border. Sew the top and bottom border strips to the quilt top, aligning the corner seams. Press toward the border.

Alternative Fabric Selection

It is always fun to flip the values around in a quilt and see how different the design looks. Make a quilt that will match its historical roots by using 1930s reproduction prints and colors instead of the bright tone-on-tone prints. Reverse the values by substituting beige or white in place of the bright prints with black backgrounds.

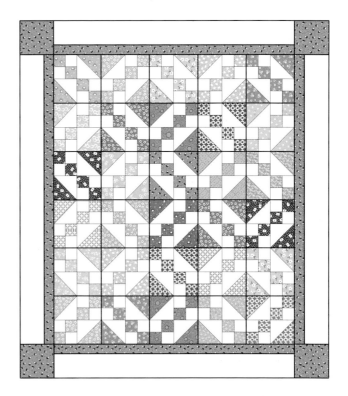

6. Layer the pieced backing, batting, and quilt top. Baste the layers together.

7. Quilt as desired.

8. Prepare the binding and sew it to the quilt.

27

Autumn Roads

Made by Shelley Nelson. Quilted by Janice Nelson, 2003.
Finished quilt size: 60½" x 60½". Finished block size: 8".

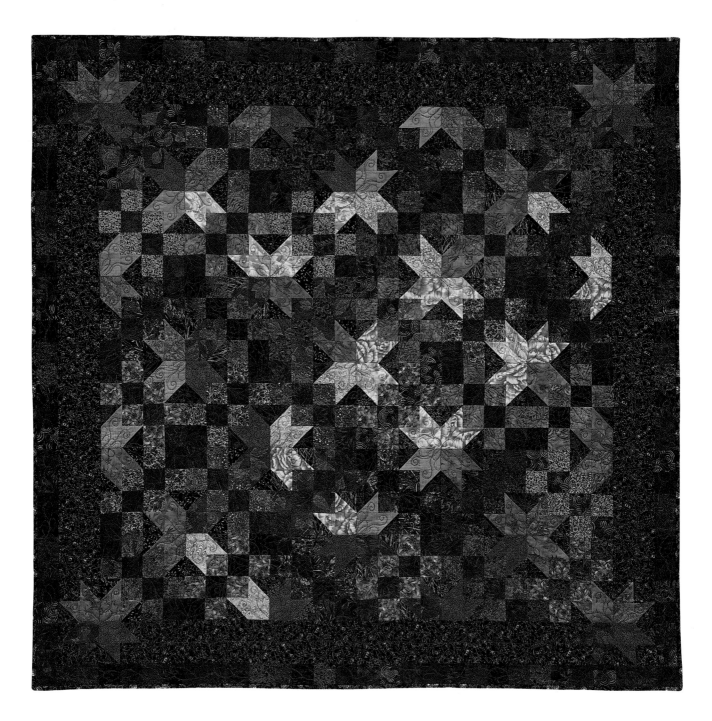

The upper Midwest, where I spent my childhood, is blessed with incredibly beautiful autumns—much like New England. The days are crisp and clear, the leaves scrunch underfoot, and the entire landscape, from the grasses to the tips of the trees, is filled with color. This quilt makes me want to grab a glass of fresh apple cider and go scuffle through some leaves. Shelley is adept at getting the most visual impact out of her fabrics; she uses eye-catching reds to form diagonal chains across the quilt and shades of gold and yellow to create the stars. Each Road to Oklahoma block forms only partial stars, and when the blocks are set block-to-block (side by side with no sashing), the stars would normally appear to be chopped off at the edges of the quilt.

To visually complete the design and add to the diagonal movement of the pattern, Shelley continued four of the stars into the inner border with some additional piecing.

Successful Fabric Selection

Choose 10 red prints. The quilt will be much more interesting if the red hues are not identical. Some may be brick red, and others could lean toward burgundy. Most of the red prints should look like a solid or mottled red from a distance and be of roughly similar values. Additionally, select nine prints in medium to medium-dark values that make you think of fall. These are for the squares on either side of the center red chain. The fabrics Shelley used are rich shades of brown, rust, and gold but have flashes of blue, purple, and green. Some of them are lighter in value than the reds and some are similar in value. Next, choose eight gold or yellow fabrics for the stars. Compared to your other fabrics, these are the lightest in value. If you look at Shelley's quilt, you will see a wide range of value and hue—everything from a medium-value orange to a pale yellow. Finally, find six fairly dark prints for the triangles that touch the gold stars. Shelley used prints with dark or black backgrounds and medium- to small-scale patterns. These are the darkest fabrics in the quilt. Use your favorite of these dark prints for the inner border.

Materials

Yardage is based on 42"-wide fabric.

1 yard of a print with black background for blocks and inner border

¼ yard each of 10 red prints for blocks and outer border

¼ yard each of 9 fall prints for blocks

¼ yard each of 8 gold or yellow prints for blocks and inner border

⅛ yard each of 5 additional prints with black background for blocks

3¾ yards for backing (2 widths pieced either vertically or horizontally)

⅝ yard for binding

65" x 65" piece of batting

Cutting

Note: Strips are cut across the width of the fabric unless indicated otherwise.

From each of the gold or yellow prints, cut:

1 strip, 2⅞" x 42"; crosscut into 11 squares, 2⅞" x 2⅞" (88 total, including 4 extra)

1 strip, 2½" x 42"; crosscut into 11 squares, 2½" x 2½" (88 total, including 4 extra)

From the larger piece of black-background print, cut:

2 strips, 2⅞" x 42"; crosscut into 24 squares, 2⅞" x 2⅞"

1 strip, 2½" x 2½"; crosscut into 12 squares, 2½" x 2½"

4 strips, 4½" x 40½" (If your fabric has less than 40½" of usable width or if your pieced blocks finish larger than 8" square, wait to cut your borders. You will need to cut 5 strips and piece the border to match the size of your quilt. See step 8 on page 32.)

From each of the additional black-background prints, cut:

1 strip, 2⅞" x 42"; crosscut into 12 squares, 2⅞" x 2⅞" (60 total)

From each of the red prints, cut:

2 strips, 2½" x 42"; crosscut into 26 squares, 2½" x 2½" (260 total) (Pin into 36 sets each of 4 matching squares. Set the rest aside for the outer border.)

From each of the fall prints, cut:

2 strips, 2½" x 42"; crosscut into 24 squares, 2½" x 2½" (216 total)

From the binding fabric, cut:

7 strips, 2½" x 42"

Assembly

Each block is made from the units shown below. Notice that each block has only four different fabrics: one red, one fall print, one dark background, and one gold or yellow. The 36 blocks in the quilt each have different combinations of these fabrics.

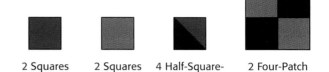

2 Squares   2 Squares   4 Half-Square-Triangle Units   2 Four-Patch Units

1. To make the half-square-triangle units, mark a diagonal line on the wrong side of each 2⅞" gold or yellow square. (Keep squares of the same fabric together to stay organized.) Layer one of these squares with a 2⅞" black-background square, right sides together. Stitch ¼" on each side of the marked line. Cut apart on the line and press toward the dark fabric. Repeat, using the same two fabrics to make four identical half-square-triangle units. Pin them together to stay organized and repeat these steps with the remaining 2⅞" squares, mixing different gold or yellow fabrics with each dark fabric. You should have 168 total units. Set aside 24 of the half-square-triangle units that contain the fabric you are using for the inner border. Keep the other triangle units grouped according to the gold or yellow fabric.

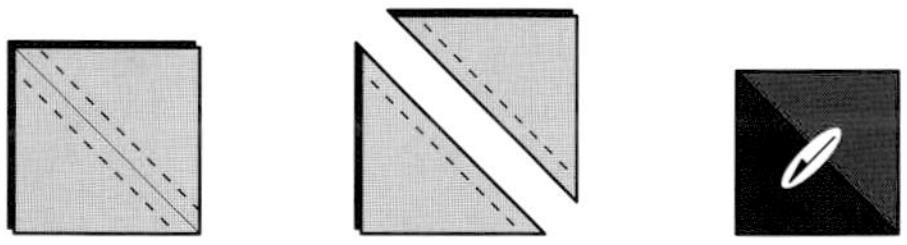

Make 168 total.

2. To make the four-patch units, sew two red squares and two fall print squares together as shown. Press toward the red fabric. Make two identical four-patch units for each block, for a total of 72. (Pin together the two identical four-patch units, and keep them grouped according to the fall print fabric.)

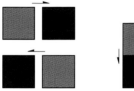

Make 2 identical units
per block (72 total).

3. Organize each block by grouping together four matching half-square-triangle units from step 1, two gold or yellow 2½" squares from the same fabric used in the triangle units, two matching four-patch units from step 2, and two 2½" squares of the same fall print used in the four-patch units. Repeat until you have 36 blocks organized. (You will have 4 unused gold or yellow squares.)

4. Working one block at a time, sew one half-square-triangle unit to a matching gold or yellow 2½" square. Press toward the square. Sew another half-square-triangle unit to a fall print 2½" square as shown. Press toward the square. Sew these units together and press. Repeat to make two star units for each block.

Make 2 identical units
per block (72 total).

5. Arrange the two star units from step 4 with the two matching four-patch units as shown. Sew the units together, being careful that the gold or yellow squares are on diagonally opposite corners and the red squares are on the other two corners. Press. Repeat to make 36 blocks.

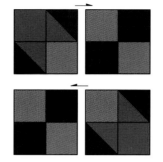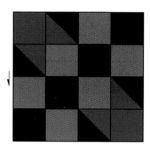

Make 36.

6. Arrange the blocks into six rows of six blocks each, rotating the blocks so that diagonal chains of red squares form and the gold or yellow star fabrics meet. Make sure each corner of the quilt has a gold or yellow square of fabric, not a red square. Sew the blocks into rows. Press rows in alternate directions and then sew the rows together. Press.

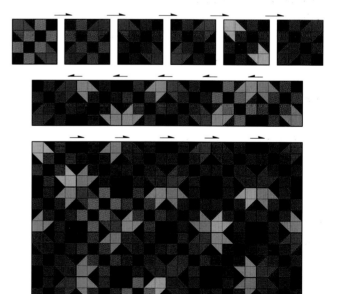

7. Make border star units from the 24 half-square triangles that were set aside in step 1 by arranging two matching half-square-triangle units, a matching gold or yellow 2½" square, and a 2½" square of the black-background print as shown. Sew the units together, being careful to position the half-square-triangle units correctly. Make 12 border star units.

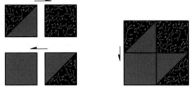

Make 12.

8. Measure the length and width of your quilt top through the center. If you have cut and sewn accurately, it should measure 48½". If your measurement is within a half inch of this, cut four inner-border strips 4½" x 40½". If your measurement is shorter than 48" or greater than 49", you will need to read the tip below and cut the long inner-border strips to fit your quilt top.

9. Sew a border star unit made in step 7 to each end of a border strip as shown, being careful to keep the gold or yellow squares in the corners. Press toward the border strip. Repeat to make two side border strips. To make the top and bottom border strips, sew two border star units to each end of the remaining inner-border strips, rotating the star units as shown. Press toward the border strips.

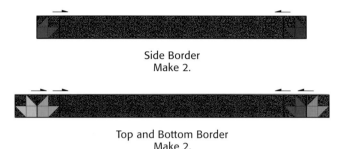

Side Border
Make 2.

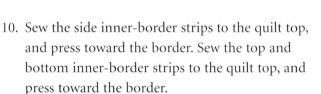

Top and Bottom Border
Make 2.

10. Sew the side inner-border strips to the quilt top, and press toward the border. Sew the top and bottom inner-border strips to the quilt top, and press toward the border.

11. Sew 28 red squares together to make one side outer-border strip. Press seams in one direction.

TIP If you are not a quilting perfectionist, your blocks may be larger or smaller than the dimension derived by computers and calculators. Usually this is not a problem, but the instructions for partially pieced borders such as this one assume that your finished blocks are the same size as what my calculator figures. You can make your borders fit perfectly by doing a little math. Begin with the measurement of the quilt top through the center and subtract ½" for the outer seam allowances. Divide this number by 6 (the number of rows in the quilt). This tells you the finished size of one of your blocks. Multiply that finished block size by 5. Add ½" for seam allowances, and that is the length you need to cut your long inner-border strips.

As an example, let's consider a top that measures 47¼". Subtract ½" for the seam allowance to get to 46¾". Divide 46¾" by 6, and the result can be rounded off to 7.79". This means each block averages 7.79" finished. Multiply 7.79" by 5, which equals 38.95", and add ½" seam allowance, which results in 39.45". You can round this number up or down to the nearest quarter inch. I tend to round up, because all the sewn seams in your quilt top allow for some ease. Completing our example, you would round up to 39½" and cut your long inner-border strips 4½" x 39½".

Compare the measurement of this pieced strip to the length of your quilt top. If necessary, take in a few seams or let out a few seams until the pieced strip is close to the length of the quilt top. Repeat to make a second side border strip the same length as the first. Sew to the sides of the quilt top, and press toward the quilt center. Sew 30 red squares together to make the top outer-border strip. Measure the width of your quilt top, and adjust the length of the pieced strip until it is close to the width of your quilt. Repeat to make the bottom outer-border strip. Sew to the top and bottom edges of the quilt. Press toward the inner border.

Alternative Fabric Selection

I think this pattern looks best if several different fabrics are used for the stars and the central chains, but you can simplify it by using just one fabric for the positions of both the fall prints and the black-background prints. This would also make a wonderful red-white-and-blue summertime quilt.

Making changes in value placement and simplifying the background can create a very different quilt.

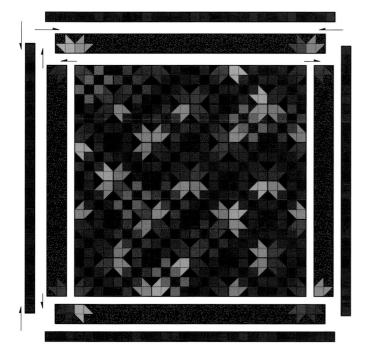

12. Layer the pieced backing, batting, and quilt top. Baste the layers together.
13. Quilt as desired.
14. Prepare the binding and sew it to the quilt.

Wisconsin Cold Snap

Made by Robin Strobel. Quilted by Pam Clarke, 2003.
Finished quilt size: 54½" x 72½". Finished block size: 9".

In the Pacific Northwest, winter is a time of misty gray days, soft rains, and weeks without seeing the sun. This is very different from my childhood home in Wisconsin. There, winters can be long and harsh, and the temperatures so cold that the sun brings light but no warmth. I am happy to miss out on the weeks of bitter cold, but I think wistfully of the bright sunshine. I dream of impossibly blue skies, brilliant white snow, and trees casting long indigo shadows. In typical Midwestern understatement, the folks in that region talk about a "little cold snap" when the high temperature for the day reaches only −5° F. The traditional Jacob's Ladder block is a perfect setting for the blue and white flannel quilt that warms my memories of a "Wisconsin Cold Snap." I did not feel this quilt needed borders, so I just bound it with the dark blue.

Successful Fabric Selection

Fabric selection for this quilt is not complicated. Choose just three fabrics—a light background, a medium for the squares, and a dark for the triangles. The three fabrics should create a strong contrast; you don't want them to blend when placed together. For a sharp, clear pattern like my sample, choose tone-on-tones, solids, or fabrics with a small print. If you want a softer-looking quilt, use a medium-scale print for one of the fabrics.

Materials

Because many flannel fabrics are narrower in width, yardage and cutting amounts are based on 40"-wide fabric.

2⅞ yards of white flannel snowflake print for blocks

1⅝ yards of medium blue flannel for blocks

1¾ yards of dark blue flannel for blocks and binding

3½ yards for backing (2 widths pieced horizontally)

59" x 77" piece of batting

Cutting

Note: Strips are cut across the width of the fabric unless indicated otherwise.

From the medium blue flannel, cut:
24 strips, 2" x 40"

From the white flannel, cut:
24 strips, 2" x 40"
5 strips, 7¾" x 40"; crosscut into 24 squares, 7¾" x 7¾"

From the dark blue flannel, cut:
5 strips, 7¾" x 40"; crosscut into 24 squares, 7¾" x 7¾"
7 strips, 2½" x 40"

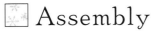 Assembly

Each block is made using the following units:

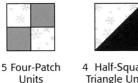

5 Four-Patch
Units

4 Half-Square-
Triangle Units

1. To make the four-patch units, sew a medium blue strip to a white strip along the long edges. Press toward the blue. Cut the strips into 2" segments. Make 24 strip sets, and cut a total of 480 segments.

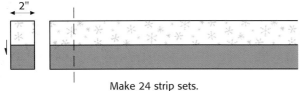

Make 24 strip sets.
Cut 480 segments.

2. Sew two of the segments from step 1 together, with center seams opposing. Press to one side. Repeat with the remaining segments to make 240 four-patch units.

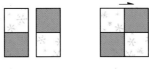

Make 240.

3. To make the half-square-triangle units, mark an X from corner to corner on the wrong side of a white square. Layer this square with a dark blue square, right sides together. Sew ¼" on each side of the marked lines. Cut the squares first vertically and then horizontally through the center (3⅞" from the edges). Be careful to make accurate cuts. Cut each piece diagonally on the marked lines and press seams toward the dark fabric. Repeat with the remaining squares to

make 192 half-square-triangle units. Press seams toward the dark blue.

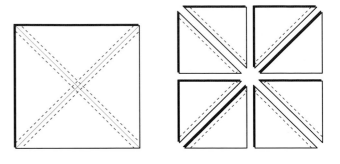

Make 192.

4. To assemble the blocks, arrange five four-patch units and four half-square-triangle units as shown. Be careful to position the medium blue squares and the dark blue triangles correctly. Sew the units into rows. Press toward the four-patch units. Sew the rows together and press as shown. Make 48.

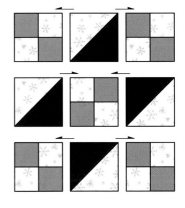

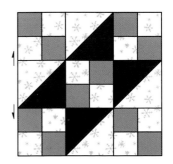

Make 48.

5. Arrange the 48 blocks as shown. Sew the blocks into rows and press the seams open. Sew the rows together and press.

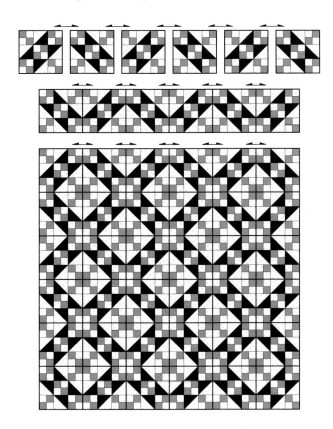

Alternative Fabric Selection

Try switching the values around, choosing a dark floral fabric to substitute for the white snowflake print, a medium value for the blue squares, and a bright, light fabric for the dark blue triangles.

6. Layer the pieced backing, batting, and quilt top. Baste the layers together.

7. Quilt as desired.

8. Prepare the binding and sew it to the quilt.

Reversing the value placement gives a different, three-dimensional effect.

Spring Fling

Made by Robin Strobel. Quilted by Pam Clarke, 2003.
Finished quilt size: 57½" x 72". Finished block size: 7¼".

Kaleidoscope is a traditional block, and this is a classic quilt in timeless colors. The illusion of overlapping dark and light circles continually draws your eyes across the surface. There are actually two variations of the block in this quilt, with the lights and darks placed in opposite positions. The center units are identical, but one block has light corners, and the other has dark corners.

Successful Fabric Selection

Like many of the quilts in this book, the relative value of the fabrics is the element that creates the design in this quilt. The greater the difference in value between the lights and darks, the more striking the pattern. I did not want the secondary pattern to be too strong, so my "dark" fabrics are prints that I actually consider to be more medium than dark in value. What is important is that the "dark" fabrics look darker in value than the "light" fabrics. I chose 16 lights and 16 darks, predominantly in cheerful blue and yellow floral prints plus a geometric or two added for variety. You can use fewer fabrics—in fact this quilt is very striking made with only one light and one dark fabric.

Be careful if you choose large prints with both dark and light areas, because their values may shift when they are cut into triangles. I used two prints that looked dark as large pieces, but some of the triangles I cut turned out to look more like my light triangles. You can still use this type of fabric—just cut extra triangles and discard any that appear to shift in value. If you make a quilt similar to mine, be aware that the color yellow usually reads light in value. Dark fabrics can have yellow in them, but if yellow is dominant, the fabric usually will read as a light.

Materials

Yardage is based on 42"-wide fabric.

1⅜ yards of floral print for outer border

⅜ yard of dark blue for inner border

¼ yard each of 16 different light fabrics for blocks (Fat quarters work well.)

¼ yard each of 16 different dark fabrics for blocks (Fat quarters work well.)

3½ yards for backing (2 widths pieced horizontally)

½ yard for binding

62" x 76" piece of batting

Template plastic or a "kaleidoscope" ruler (This type of ruler can be found in most quilt shops.)

Cutting

Note: Strips are cut across the width of the fabric unless indicated otherwise.

From each of the 16 light and 16 dark fabrics, cut:
1 strip, 4½" x 42" (If using fat quarters, cut 2 strips, 4½" x 21", from each.)

From the dark blue, cut:
6 strips, 1¾" x 42"

From the floral print, cut:
6 strips, 6" x 42" (My outer-border fabric was not a full 42" wide, so I had to cut 7 strips.)

From the binding fabric, cut:
7 strips, 2¼" x 42"

 Assembly

Each block is made using the following units:

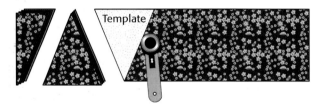

4 Light and 4 Dark
Center Triangles

4 Light or Dark
Corner Triangles

1. From each strip (or strips) of light and dark fabric, cut 12 large triangles using either a template made from the pattern provided on page 43, or a "kaleidoscope" ruler. Refer to page 11 in the "Cutting" section of "Quilting Basics" for more on using templates. To keep the drudgery at a minimum, I layer several strips and cut about six triangles at a time. You will have a total of 192 dark triangles and 192 light triangles.

Cut 192 dark triangles
and 192 light triangles.

2. From the remainder of each light and dark strip, cut three 3½" squares. You will have a total of 48 light squares and 48 dark squares. Cut each square in half on the diagonal. Set aside.

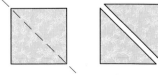

Cut 96.

Cut 96.

3. Randomly select a large light and a large dark triangle cut in step 1 and place right sides together. Stitch along one long bias edge. Repeat to sew each large light triangle to a large dark triangle. It does not matter if you sew with the light or the dark fabric on the top, but you need to be consistent. Keep the same value of fabric on the top! Press toward the dark fabric, being careful not to stretch the bias edges. Trim the "dog ears."

Start.

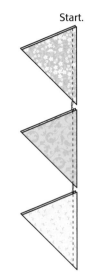
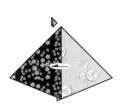

Press toward dark.
Trim "ears."

TIP The bias edges are very stretchy, so be careful not to tug or pull on the fabric as you stitch. I find it easiest to begin stitching at the wider corner. If I don't, my machine tends to swallow thin points into the bobbin assembly and then choke on the resulting wad of fabric (especially if I have not changed my needle recently).

4. Randomly pair two of the units made in step 3. The light and dark triangles should alternate, and the pressed seams should nestle together, making it easier to match the seams at the points. Stitch along one long edge. Press toward

the dark fabric. Repeat with the remaining units made in step 3. Make 96 units.

Make 96.

TIP It is hard for us control freaks to do something totally randomly, but don't try to control which fabrics are paired. The only criterion I used was to not repeat the same fabric within the center portion of a block. (Well, I also didn't want two bird prints together, and there were two floral prints that I didn't want together, and then there was the light blue checkerboard and the blue and yellow plaid that I didn't want together, and . . .) Trust me. Don't make yourself crazy here. Try to just randomly sew the pairs together.

5. Sew together two of the units made in step 4. This is the trickiest step in constructing the blocks, because you have to match the points of eight different triangles. (See "General Piecing" on page 13.) Press the seam open to reduce bulk. You will get a "pie-plate" shape of eight triangles that will become the center of a block. Repeat with the remaining large triangle units to make 48 center units.

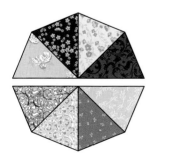

Make 48.

6. Roughly center a small dark triangle cut in step 2 against a large light triangle of a center unit and sew as shown. The corners of the small triangle will extend past the sides of the center unit. (It is difficult to perfectly center the corner triangles, so they are cut oversized and the corners will be trimmed.) Stitch ¼" from the edge. Repeat, sewing a small dark triangle to each of the remaining three large light triangles in the center unit. Press toward the small triangles. Trim the corners even with the center unit, being careful to leave a ¼" seam allowance where the seams cross. Your block should measure approximately 7¼". (Do not panic if your measurements are a little off. Fabric stretches!) Repeat this step on half of the center units to make 24 blocks with dark corners.

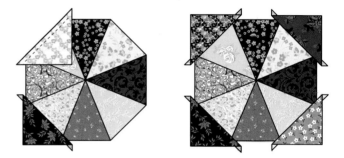

7. Repeat step 6, this time sewing four small light corner triangles to the large dark triangles. Press and trim. Make 24 blocks with light corners.

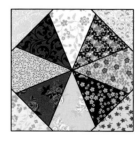

Make 24.

8. Arrange the blocks into eight rows of six blocks each, alternating light-cornered and dark-cornered blocks. Sew the blocks into rows, matching points where triangles join. Press

seams in alternate directions from row to row. Sew the rows together, again matching triangle points. I admit it: My blocks were not perfect, and I had to ease a little and stretch a little to get the seams to line up. If you have trouble, see "General Piecing" on page 13 for tips. Press. If you could bring your face right up against my quilt, you might be tempted to examine every single point to be certain it matches perfectly. Since you can't see it that closely, I'm going to go with a "don't ask, don't tell" policy.

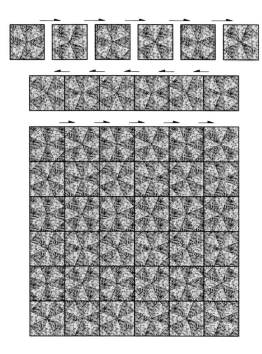

9. Sew the 1¾" dark blue inner-border strips end to end to make one long strip. Press. Measure the length of the quilt top through the center and cut two border strips to this size. Sew the strips to the sides of the quilt top, matching centers and easing as needed. The points in the quilt top will be easier to match if you sew with the quilt on top and the border strips underneath. Press toward the border. Measure the width of the quilt top through the center and cut two border strips to this size. Sew to the top and bottom of the quilt, matching centers and easing as needed. Press toward the border.

10. Sew the 6" floral outer-border strips end to end to make one long strip. Press. Measure the length of the quilt top through the center and cut two border strips to this size. Sew to the sides of the quilt top. Press toward the outer border. Measure the width of the quilt top through the center and cut two border strips to this size. Sew to the top and bottom of the quilt. Press toward the outer border.

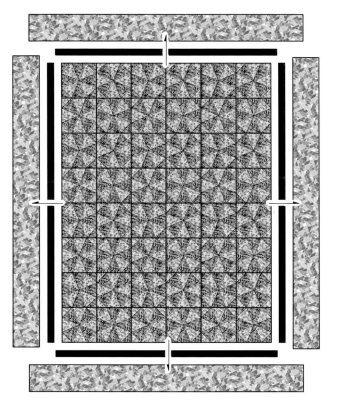

11. Layer the pieced backing, batting, and quilt top. Baste the layers together.

12. Quilt as desired.

13. Prepare the binding and sew it to the quilt.

Alternative Fabric Selection

This pattern looks great using just about any style of fabric or color scheme. Remember to keep a visual distinction between the light and dark values, and the secondary pattern will always be visible. Often a kaleidoscope quilt is made with just one light and one dark fabric. It would be stunning with a beautiful dark Christmas print and a white or off-white tone-on-tone print.

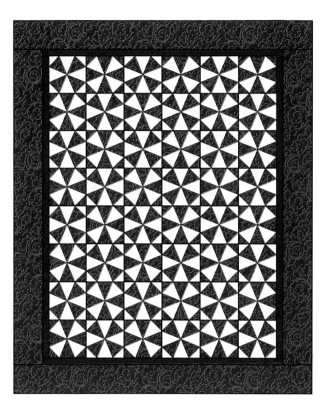

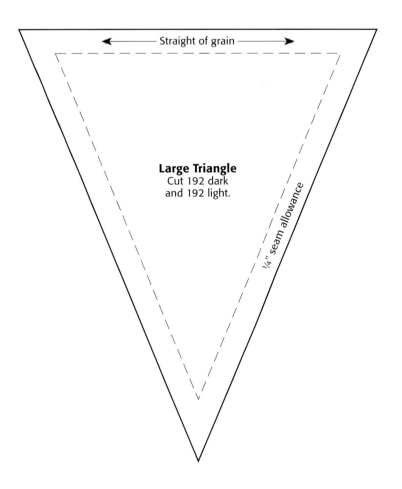

Straight of grain

Large Triangle
Cut 192 dark
and 192 light.

¼" seam allowance

Butterfly Garden

Made by Robin Strobel. Quilted by Pam Clarke, 2003.
Finished quilt size: 58½" x 58½". Finished block size: 8".

In my first attempt at this Sawtooth Star variation, I used only three fabrics and had a different placement of lights and darks. I was dismayed to find that the secondary designs completely dominated the quilt top and the stars became totally invisible! Convinced that this block could make a striking pattern, I redesigned the quilt, shifting the values around and using different colors for the star points to keep them a soft but distinct part of the design. This variation forms a three-dimensional illusion as a secondary pattern and has become one of my favorite quilts.

Successful Fabric Selection

Find a small- to medium-scale print fabric with a light to medium value to be your feature print. Use the range of colors in your feature print as a starting point to choose 12 medium-value tone-on-tone prints or solids for the stars. These should be colors that gradate across the color wheel from one hue to another. It's OK (and even more interesting) if some of the tone-on-tone fabrics are not colors included in your feature print. As long as some of the colors are included, the rest should blend nicely. (I confess, I actually reversed this process. I first purchased hand-dyed fabric* for the star points and then stumbled across the butterfly print at the fabric store.) Finally, choose a dark background fabric to provide dramatic contrast to the print and tonal fabrics. If you want to simplify the pattern, you can use just six different medium-value fabrics for the star points. Purchase a quarter yard of each of the six fabrics. Just change the instructions to make 24 flying-geese units from each color (six blocks).

*For hand-dyed fabrics that gradate across the color wheel, visit Starr Designs at www.starrfabrics.com, P.O. Box 440, Etna, CA 96027

Materials

Yardage is based on 42"-wide fabric.

2¼ yards of dark purple background fabric for blocks and inner border

2⅛ yards of medium to light feature print for blocks, outer border, and binding

Fat eighth each of 12 different medium tone-on-tone prints or hand-dyed fabrics for blocks

3½ yards for backing (2 widths pieced vertically or horizontally)

63" x 63" piece of batting

Cutting

Note: Strips are cut across the width of the fabric unless indicated otherwise.

From the feature print, cut:
9 strips, 2½" x 42"; cut 4½ of the strips into 72 squares, 2½" x 2½"
6 strips, 4½" x 42"
7 strips, 2½" x 42"

From the purple background fabric, cut:
9 strips, 2½" x 42"; cut 4½ of the strips into 72 squares, 2½" x 2½"
9 strips, 4½" x 42"; crosscut into 144 rectangles, 2½" x 4½"
5 strips, 1½" x 42"

From each tone-on-tone print, cut:
3 strips, 2½" x 20"; crosscut into 24 squares, 2½" x 2½" (288 total)

 Assembly

Each block is made using the following units:

2 Squares   2 Squares   4 Flying-Geese Units   1 Four-Patch Unit

1. To make the four-patch units, sew a 2½" feature-print strip to a 2½" dark strip along the long edges. Press toward the dark fabric. Crosscut into segments 2½" wide. Repeat with the remaining 2½" strips of each fabric to make 72 segments.

Make 4½ strip sets.
Cut 72 segments.

2. Sew two of the segments from step 1 together as shown. Press the seam to one side. Repeat with the remaining segments to make 36 four-patch units.

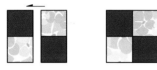

Make 36.

3. To make the flying-geese units, mark a diagonal line on the wrong side of each medium-value square. (Keep each of the 12 colors separate.) Place a marked square on the end of one of the dark rectangles, right sides together. Sew along the marked line. Press toward the corner and trim the excess fabric, leaving about ¼" seam allowance. Place a second square of the same fabric on the opposite end of the rectangle and then sew along the marked line. Press toward the corner and trim the excess. Make 12 flying-geese units from each color.

Make 12
of each combination
(144 total).

4. Arrange one four-patch unit, four flying-geese units with the same color combination, two feature-print squares, and two dark squares into a block as shown. Sew the units into rows and press as shown. Sew the rows together. Press. Make three blocks of each color combination.

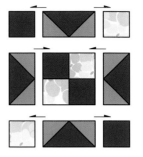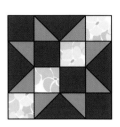

Make 3 of each
combination (36 total).

5. Arrange the blocks into six rows of six blocks each. I rotated the blocks so that the lights and darks form a diamond image, but you may like to experiment with rotating the blocks and forming different patterns. Sew the blocks into rows and press in alternate directions from row to row. Sew the rows together and press.

46

6. Sew the 1½" purple inner-border strips together end to end to make one long strip. Press. Measure the length of the quilt top through the center and cut two strips to this size. Sew these strips to each side of the quilt top. Press toward the border. Measure the width of the quilt top through the center and cut two strips to this size. Sew to the top and bottom of the quilt top. Press toward the border.

7. Sew the 4½" feature-print outer-border strips together end to end to make one long strip. Press. Measure the length of the quilt top through the center and cut two strips to this size. Sew to each side of the quilt top. Press toward the outer border. Measure the width of the quilt top through the center and cut two strips to this size. Sew to the top and bottom of the quilt top. Press toward the outer border.

8. Layer the pieced backing, batting, and quilt top. Baste the layers together.

9. Quilt as desired.

10. Prepare the binding and sew it to the quilt.

Alternative Fabric Selection

My sample quilt uses what I consider to be spring-time colors, but I'd love to see this pattern in the rich golds, russets, and browns of fall. Keep the star points in different medium-value colors, but find a dark, rich autumnal feature print and a light background.

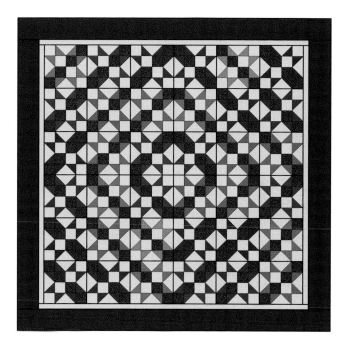

47

Karen's Puzzle

Made by Karen Soltys. Quilted by Pam Clarke, 2003.
Finished quilt size: 51½" x 63½". Finished block size: 12".

The date on this quilt is 2003, but visually it could be from 1863. When I wanted a scrappy, traditional-looking quilt for this book, I turned to Karen (and her terrific stash) for help. She has a love of antiques, gardens, textiles, and color that adds richness and history to her quilts. Most women in the 1800s could not afford large pieces of fabric. They hoarded scraps salvaged from old clothes, feed sacks, and blankets. When they had enough, they sorted them into light and dark values, and pieced them into quilts. In keeping with the era, this quilt has no solid borders. Instead, the block design was continued to finish off the dark stars on the sides of the quilt. You may know this block by several different names—Monkey Wrench, Indiana Puzzle, and Milky Way being the most common.

 ## Successful Fabric Selection

Take a look at all the different fabrics Karen used as her "lights." There is actually a wide range of values and colors. Some "lights" are quite dark, but in general they are lighter in value than the fabrics she used as "darks." The hues are warm and varied: cream, pink, tan, and green. The dark fabrics in the quilt are a little more consistent. Each of the dark stars is made from one dark and one light fabric. Each of the four-patch units is also made from one dark and one light fabric. Karen did not limit herself to reproduction prints but did choose fabrics with warm, country colors and mostly small-scale designs. She used far more than 40 different fabrics to make this sample. However, for those of us who do not have large stashes containing this type of fabric, I have simplified the materials to 20 light and 20 dark fabrics. If you have more, by all means use them.

Materials

Yardage is based on 42"-wide fabric.

¼ yard each of 20 different light prints for blocks (Fat quarters work well.)*

¼ yard each of 20 different dark prints for blocks (Fat quarters work well.)*

3¼ yards for backing (2 widths pieced horizontally)

½ yard total for binding

56" x 68" piece of batting

Fat eighths (9" x 20") are actually sufficient, but they're hard to find. Also, you would need additional fabric for the binding. If you use fat quarters, cut the excess fabric into squares and rectangles. To be thrifty like our ancestors, sew them together for the quilt back.

Cutting

Note: All strips are cut across the width of the fabric unless indicated otherwise.

From each light print, cut:
5 squares, 3⅞" x 3⅞"
10 squares, 2" x 2"
2 squares, 3½" x 3½"

From each dark print, cut:
5 squares, 3⅞" x 3⅞"
10 squares, 2" x 2"
2 squares, 3½" x 3½"

From each of 12 different prints (remainders of above), cut:
1 strip, 2½" x 21" (This is optional and is for a "scrappy" binding.)

Assembly

To provide visual consistency, each dark star is made from four identical half-square-triangle units and a center square of the same dark fabric. Each four-patch unit is made from any combination of light and dark fabrics. The four-patch units are not a problem, but a traditional Indiana Puzzle block contains one whole and three partial dark stars. (Only when the blocks are placed together do the other stars become apparent.) With this type of block, it can be confusing to attempt a scrappy quilt and ensure the correct fabric placement in the blocks. In this case, it is actually easier to spread out all the units on a work wall before you sew the units together. Make certain that the dark stars all use the same light and dark fabrics, and then sew the units into rows. Finally, sew the rows together.

Fat-Eighth Cutting Layout

Depending on whether you're using traditional quarter-yard cuts, fat quarters, or fat eighths, you'll cut your fabric in different ways. If you use fat eighths, cut carefully following the cutting diagram. There is little room for error, but if you make one and don't have enough fabric, just add another print! This is a scrap quilt—more is better.

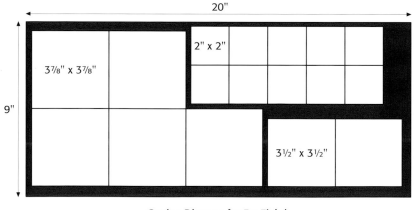

Cutting Diagram for Fat Eighth

Although you won't be sewing an actual block together, if you were, each block would be made using the following units:

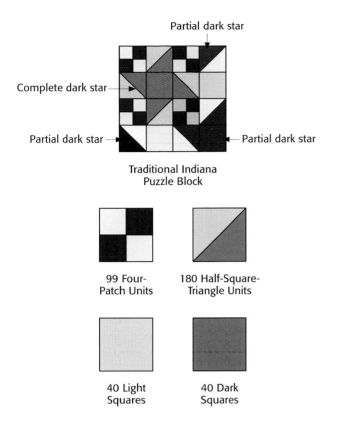

Partial dark star

Complete dark star →

Partial dark star → ← Partial dark star

Traditional Indiana
Puzzle Block

99 Four-
Patch Units

180 Half-Square-
Triangle Units

40 Light
Squares

40 Dark
Squares

1. You will need to make four identical half-square-triangle units for each dark star, as well as a couple of extras to finish the pattern at the edges of the quilt. First, keep the sets of five 3⅞" light squares together. Divide the sets of five 3⅞" dark squares into two sets of two squares each and a single remaining square. To make the half-square-triangle units, mark a diagonal line on the wrong side of each 3⅞" light square. Layer one of these squares with a dark 3⅞" square, right sides together. Stitch ¼" on each side of the marked line. Cut apart on the line and press toward the dark fabric. Repeat, using the same two fabrics to make four identical half-square-triangle units. Using the same light fabric pair it with two squares of a different dark fabric and make four more half-square-triangle units. Pair the fifth 3⅞" square of the light fabric with still another different 3⅞" dark square and make two

half-square-triangle units. Repeat these steps with all the remaining 3⅞" squares. Make 40 sets of four identical half-square-triangle units and 20 sets of two identical units (200 total).

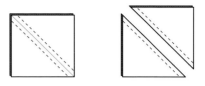

Make 40 sets of 4 identical units
and 20 sets of 2 identical units.

2. To make the four-patch units, stitch a 2" light square to a 2" dark square, right sides together. Press toward the dark fabric. Repeat with two more squares of the same fabrics, and sew together as shown. Press. Repeat with the remaining 2" light and dark squares. Make 100.

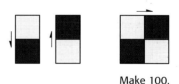

Make 100.

3. Arrange the half-square-triangle units, four-patch units, and 3½" squares into rows. (You will have some half-square-triangle units and one four-patch unit left over.) I find it easiest to use a work wall. I first arrange the four half-square-triangle units and matching dark square that form each dark star, leaving gaps for the four-patch units and light squares. Then I place the light squares on the work wall, and play the game of musical squares—trying to keep the same light fabric from touching itself. Finally I add the four-patch units, once again trying to keep the fabrics nicely mixed, and also being very careful to position the light and dark squares correctly. The tip of each dark star should touch a dark square. Step back and

squint at the quilt. Your eye should want to move across the surface, and not get fixated at one area. If all you can do is stare at one spot, think about what catches your eye and rearrange the fabrics to break up the pattern. I find it easiest if I then take the time to attach a small piece of masking tape with a number and

letter indicating the row and placement on the upper left corner of each unit (but not right at the edge—you don't want the tape to get caught in a seam). For example, the first row of units would be marked 1a, 1b, 1c, etc., up to 1q. Sew the units into rows and press away from the half-square-triangle units. Sew the rows together.

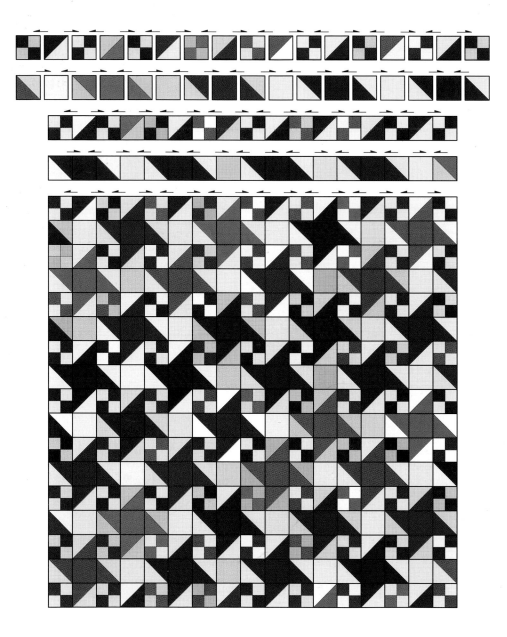

4. Layer the pieced backing, batting, and quilt top. Baste the layers together.

5. Quilt as desired.

6. Prepare the binding and sew it to the quilt. You can either use one fabric for the binding, or piece a "scrappy" binding using the twelve 2½" strips.

Alternative Fabric Selection

You can make this quilt with just two fabrics or with one fabric for the background and an assortment of fabrics for contrast. There is a multitude of beautiful styles and choices that work well with this pattern. Just make sure the "darks" and "lights" are distinctly different from each other so that the pieces don't visually blur together.

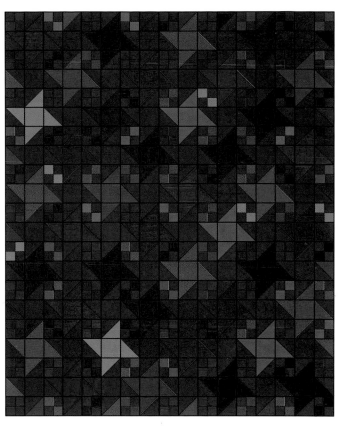

Choose bright children's prints for a fun, contemporary quilt.

Two fabrics, a floral and a contrasting solid, create a striking design.

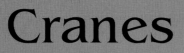

Cranes

Made by Robin Strobel. Quilted by Janice Nelson, 2003.
Finished quilt size: 64½" x 64½". Finished block size: 12".

Sometimes I choose a pattern and then the fabric, but with this quilt I fell in love with the colors and elegance of the Asian-style print first. I then went hunting for a block that could showcase the fabric and also form an intriguing secondary pattern. I found what I was looking for in this variation of the traditional Bachelor's Puzzle block. The crane fabric forms a wonderful background for the lattice and squares. I was careful to keep all the cranes flying "up" in the border and center squares, but I let them fly any which way in the small corner triangles. The perfectionist part of my soul cringes about those corners! However, I know I would have driven myself crazy figuring out how to cut and sew the blocks, plus focusing my attention enough to sew it all together correctly. I try to put my time and energy into the details that are most important to me. I was able to convince myself that with such small corner triangles, not enough of the print shows to determine the position of anything recognizable. You can judge for yourself.

Successful Fabric Selection

Build the quilt around a medium- or large-scale print that you want to use as the main visual feature. The two coordinating tone-on-tone fabrics that form the secondary lattice pattern across the quilt top are both in the same color family, with one lighter in value than the other. The small squares in the block can be any fabric that contrasts well against the tone-on-tones. I auditioned about six fabrics for these squares—everything from dark and light blues to peach—before settling on the dark burgundy print. A fabric that contrasts strongly with the others will make the squares appear to leap off the surface of the block and give a great three-dimensional illusion, but it will also pull attention from the featured print. I chose a fabric that is darker in value than the others, but in similar colors. Using an active print softens the contrast. The inner border can easily be made from one of the fabrics used in the blocks, but I wanted to bring out the blue in my feature print, and so I found a pretty tone-on-tone that did the job.

Materials

Yardage is based on 42"-wide fabric.

2½ yards of feature print for blocks and outer border (If using a directional fabric, you will need 2⅝ yards.)

1½ yards of gold tone-on-tone print for blocks and binding

1¼ yards of cinnamon tone-on-tone print for blocks

¾ yard of burgundy print for blocks

¼ yard of medium blue print for inner border

4 yards of backing (2 widths pieced either vertically or horizontally)

69" x 69" piece of batting

Cutting

Note: All strips are cut across the width of the fabric unless indicated otherwise.

From the cinnamon print, cut:

6 strips, 3½" x 42"; crosscut into 64 squares, 3½" x 3½"

2 strips, 7¾" x 42"; crosscut into 8 squares, 7¾" x 7¾"

From the feature print*, cut:

3 strips, 6½" x 42"; crosscut into 16 squares, 6½" x 6½"

2 strips, 7¾" x 42"; crosscut into 8 squares, 7¾" x 7¾"

6 strips, 7½" x 42"

*If the feature print is directional, you will need to cut the side borders along the length of the fabric, instead of crosswise selvage-to-selvage. Follow the diagram at right for cutting a directional print.

From the gold print, cut:

4 strips, 7¾" x 42"; crosscut into 16 squares, 7¾" x 7¾"

7 strips, 2½" x 42"

From the burgundy print, cut:

6 strips, 3½" x 42"; crosscut into 64 squares, 3½" x 3½"

From the medium blue print, cut:

5 strips, 1½" x 42"

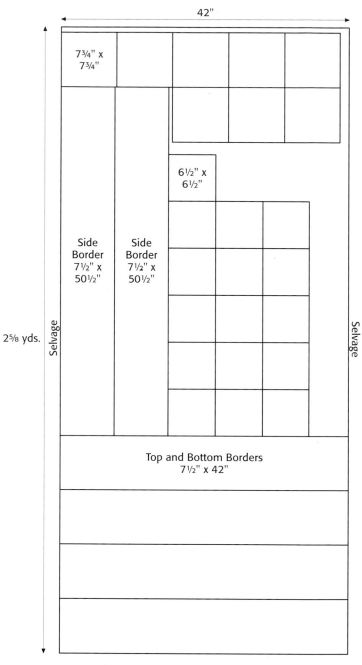

Cutting Diagram for One-Way Design Feature Print

56

◼ Assembly

Each block is made using the following units:

1 Square-in-a-Square
Center Unit

4 Cinnamon/Gold
Half-Square-
Triangle units

4 Feature-Print/Gold
Half-Square-
Triangle Units

4 Squares

1. To make the center square-in-a-square units, place a 3½" cinnamon square on a corner of a 6½" square of feature print, right sides together. Stitch diagonally across the cinnamon square as shown. Trim the corner, leaving a ¼" seam allowance. Press toward the cinnamon corner. In the same manner, sew cinnamon squares to the other three corners of the 6½" square. Trim and press toward the corners. Repeat with the remaining 6½" feature-print squares and the 3½" cinnamon squares. Make 16.

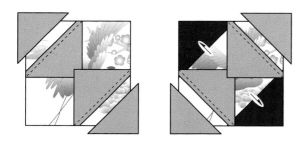

Make 16.

2. To make the cinnamon/gold half-square-triangle units, first mark an X on the wrong side of a 7¾" gold square. Layer this square with a 7¾" cinnamon square, right sides together. Sew ¼" on each side of the drawn lines. Cut the squares first vertically and then horizontally through the center (3⅞" from the edges). Be careful to make accurate cuts. Cut each piece diagonally on the marked lines and press seams toward the cinnamon. Repeat with the remaining 7¾" cinnamon squares. Make 64.

 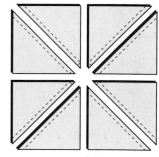

Make 64.

3. To make the feature-print/gold half-square-triangle units, first mark an X on the wrong side of a 7¾" feature-print square. Layer the square with a 7¾" gold square, right sides together. Pin to keep the squares from shifting and stitch ¼" on either side of the drawn lines. Cut the squares, first vertically and then horizontally through the center (3⅞" from the edges). Be careful to make accurate cuts. Cut each piece diagonally on the marked lines and press seams

toward the gold. Repeat with the remaining 7¾"
feature-print squares. Make 64.

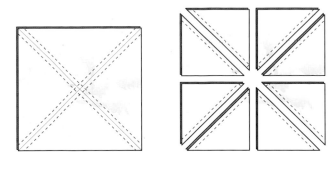

Make 64.

4. Arrange a square-in-a-square center unit, four
   cinnamon/gold half-square-triangle units, four
   feature-print/gold half-square-triangle units,
   and four 3½" burgundy squares as shown. Sew
   the units into rows, and press. Sew the rows
   together and press as shown. Make 16 blocks.

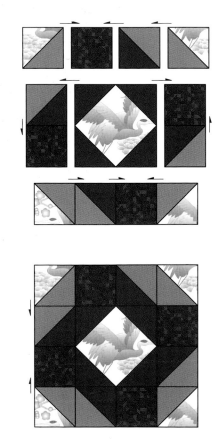

Make 16.

5. Arrange the blocks in four rows of four blocks
   each. If you are using a directional feature fabric, check to be sure that all blocks are positioned correctly. Sew the blocks into rows. Press
   in alternate directions from row to row and then
   sew the rows together. Press.

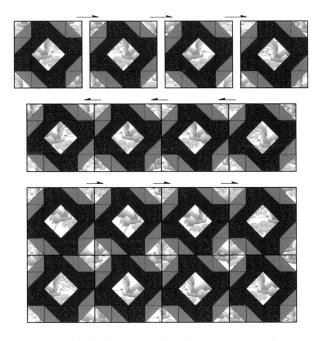

6. Sew the 1½" blue inner-border strips together
   end to end to make one long strip. Measure the
   length of the quilt top through the center. Cut
   two border strips to this size. Sew to each side
   of the quilt top and press toward the border.
   Measure the width of the quilt top through the
   center. Cut two border strips to this size. Sew
   to the top and bottom of the quilt and press
   toward the border.

7. If you are using a non-directional print for the
   outer border, sew the six 7½" outer-border
   strips end to end to make one long strip.
   Measure and cut as in step 6.

8. If you are using a directional print, measure the
   length of the quilt top through the center *before*
   you sew the side borders (previously cut) to
   both sides of the quilt. Make any necessary
   adjustments. Sew the side outer-border strips to
   the quilt and press toward the outer border. Sew
   the top and bottom outer-border strips end to
   end. Measure the width of the quilt top through

the center. Cut two border strips to this measurement. Sew to the top and bottom of the quilt and press toward the outer border.

9. Layer the pieced backing, batting, and quilt top. Baste the layers together.

10. Quilt as desired.

11. Prepare the binding and sew it to the quilt.

Alternative Fabric Selection

Choose a dark-value print for the background, medium and medium-light prints for the cinnamon and gold fabrics, and something bright in place of

the burgundy squares. You can make this pattern look very different just by reversing the values.

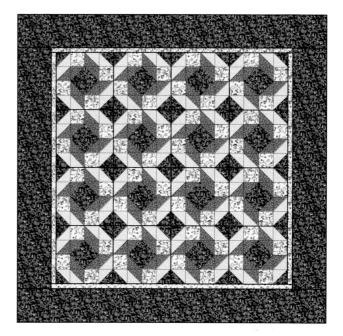

One block can have many design possibilities. This is still the same Bachelor's Puzzle block. I changed the background and burgundy square fabrics to a plain white. The blue fabrics remain the same as in the above example.

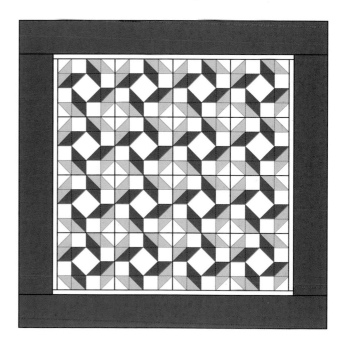

Regina's Mosaic

Made by Regina Girard. Quilted by Pam Clarke, 2003.
Finished quilt size: 54½" x 64½". Finished block size: 10".

The Mosaic block probably dates back to the 1930s, but you'd never guess it from this contemporary-looking quilt. I love the juxtaposition of peach and pink with deep purple and rust. Regina is a book designer for Martingale & Company, and her great sense of color and design is certainly apparent in her quilts.

 ## Successful Fabric Selection

The colors in the sample quilt are so beautiful that it is hard to see past them to the values that really drive the design. First, choose a light/medium-value print that you just can't live without for the center square of the block. This is a good place to highlight a medium- to large-scale print, because the square is fairly large. (It would also be a nice place for a fussy-cut motif.) Next, find a slightly darker tone-on-tone print and a very light tone-on-tone print that have similar hues to your first fabric. In Regina's quilt these are the medium-dark fuchsia and the light pink prints. Choose another color that is in your first print, and find a very dark tone-on-tone fabric in that hue. The remaining two fabrics are medium and medium-dark prints that are almost interchangeable.

Materials

Yardage is based on 42"-wide fabric.

2⅜ yards of very dark purple tone-on-tone for blocks, outer border, and binding

1¼ yards of medium-dark plum print for blocks

1¼ yards of medium-dark fuchsia tone-on-tone print for blocks

¾ yard of light pink tone-on-tone print for blocks and inner border

⅝ yard of medium-light pink print for center squares of blocks

½ yard of medium plum tone-on-tone print for blocks

3½ yards for backing (2 widths pieced horizontally)

59" x 69" piece of batting

Cutting

Note: All strips are cut across the width of the fabric unless indicated otherwise.

From the very dark purple, cut:
7 strips, 3" x 42"; crosscut into 80 squares, 3" x 3"
6 strips, 6" x 42"
7 strips, 2½" x 42"

From the medium-light pink print, cut:
3 strips, 5½" x 42"; crosscut into 20 squares, 5½" x 5½"

From the medium-dark fuchsia print, cut:
13 strips, 3" x 42"; crosscut into 160 squares, 3" x 3"

From the medium-dark plum print, cut:
7 strips, 5½" x 42"; crosscut into 80 rectangles, 3" x 5½"

From the light pink print, cut:
2 strips, 6¾" x 42"; crosscut into 10 squares, 6¾" x 6¾"
5 strips, 2" x 42"

From the medium plum print, cut:
2 strips, 6¾" x 42"; crosscut into 10 squares, 6¾" x 6¾"

 # Assembly

Each block is made using the following units:

1 Square-in-a-Square   4 Flying-Geese   4 Half-Square-
Unit   Units   Triangle Units

1. To make the square-in-a-square units, mark a diagonal line on the wrong side of each 3" dark purple square. Place one of these squares on one corner of a 5½" medium-light pink square, right sides together. Stitch diagonally across the purple square as shown. Trim the corner, leaving a ¼" seam allowance. Press toward the purple. In the same manner, sew dark purple squares to the other three corners of the pink square. Trim and press toward the corners. Repeat with the remaining purple squares and medium-light pink squares. Make 20.

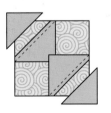

Make 20.

2. To make the flying-geese units, mark a diagonal line on the wrong side of each fuchsia square. Place one of these squares on one end of a medium-dark plum rectangle. Sew from corner to corner as shown and trim the excess, leaving about ¼" seam allowance. Press toward the corner. Sew a second fuchsia square to the other end of the rectangle as shown. Trim, and press toward the corner. Repeat to make 80 flying-geese units.

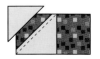

Make 80.

3. To make the half-square-triangle units, mark an X from corner to corner on the wrong side of a 6¾" light pink square. Layer this square with a medium plum square, right sides together. Sew ¼" on each side of the marked lines. Cut the squares first vertically and then horizontally through the center (3⅜" from the edges). Be careful to make accurate cuts. Cut each piece diagonally on the marked lines and press seams toward the plum fabric. Repeat with the remaining 6¾" squares. Make 80.

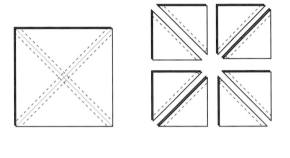

Make 80.

4. Arrange one square-in-a-square unit, four flying-geese units, and four half-square-triangle units as shown. Sew the blocks into rows, press the rows in opposite directions, and sew the rows together. I press the seams open, but you can press the rows in alternate directions if you prefer. Repeat to make 20 blocks.

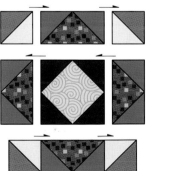 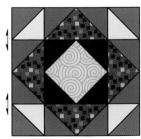

Make 20.

5. Arrange the blocks into five rows of four blocks each. Sew the blocks into rows and press seams in opposite directions from row to row. Sew the rows together and press.

6. Sew the 2" light pink inner-border strips end to end to make one long strip. Measure the length of the quilt top through the center and cut two border strips to this size. Sew a strip to each side of the quilt top. Press toward the border. Measure the width of the quilt top through the center and cut two border strips to this size. Sew the strips to the top and bottom of the quilt top. Press toward the border.

7. Sew the 6" purple outer-border strips end to end to make one long strip. Measure the length of the quilt top through the center and cut two border strips to this size. Sew to each side of the quilt top. Press toward the outer border. Measure the width of the quilt top through the center and cut two border strips to this size. Sew to the top and bottom of the quilt top. Press toward the outer border.

8. Layer the pieced backing, batting, and quilt top. Baste the layers together.

9. Quilt as desired.

10. Prepare the binding and sew it to the quilt.

■ Alternative Fabric Selection

Try switching the values around and choosing fabrics from an entirely different color palette such as country blues and browns. Or fussy cut a fun novelty print for the center squares, and choose bright fabrics to show it off. Your quilt may look entirely different from my sample, but as long as you use fabrics in light, medium, and dark values, you will still achieve a secondary pattern.

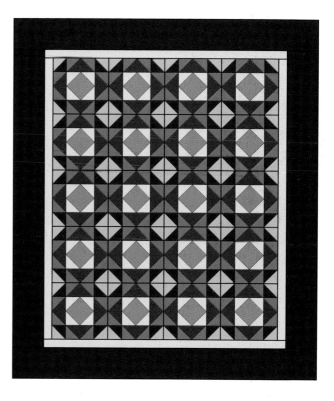

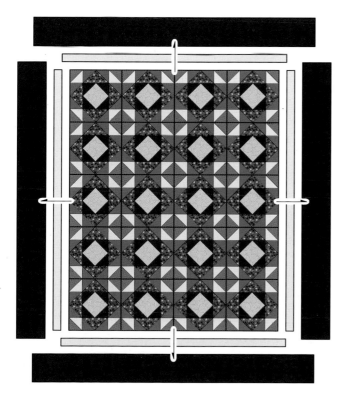

Interlocking Friendship

Made by Robin Strobel. Quilted by Pam Clarke, 2003.
Finished quilt size: 50½" x 68½". Finished block size: 9".

I love the richness of batik fabrics, and what better way to showcase them than with these twining ribbons and spinning stars? The stars in different colors are easily cut from fat quarters, so here is your excuse to indulge in those tempting packets offered by your quilt shop! The block is a combination of the traditional Ribbon Quilt block and a pattern I know only as a Friendship Star Variation. I wanted the ribbons to finish in points instead of being chopped off, so this quilt has a pieced inner border to continue the pattern. I used a plain outer border to center the design and add to the illusion of the pattern floating in space.

Successful Fabric Selection

Choose a very dark batik for the background and a very light batik for the ribbons. For the stars, look for a medium-dark and a medium-light fabric from six different color groups (12 star fabrics total). Don't worry too much about matching colors. If you like the way two fabrics look together but one has orange-red in it and the other has fire-engine red, go ahead and use them together. Look at the contrast between each pair of star fabrics, the background, and the ribbon fabrics. It is more important that the stars stand out from both the background and the ribbons than it is to see the two different fabrics in the stars. A batik fabric, when cut up, will often result in variations of color and value from piece to piece. This means that even though you use the same batik in the same position in each block, you may well achieve different looks from block to block.

Materials

Yardage is based on 42"-wide fabric.

2⅞ yards of dark blue fabric for background, pieced inner border, outer border, and binding

1½ yards of light fabric for ribbon and pieced inner border

¼ yard each of 12 different fabrics from 6 different color groups for stars—a medium-dark and a medium-light from each group*

3⅛ yards for backing (2 widths pieced horizontally)

55" x 73" piece of batting

If you can find them, you may use 12 fat eighths (9" x 20") instead.

Cutting

Note: All strips are cut across the width of the fabric unless indicated otherwise.

From each of the 12 star fabrics, cut:
1 square, 7¾" x 7¾"
8 squares, 2" x 2"
(It helps to stay organized by keeping star fabrics of the same color together.)

From the light fabric, cut:

5 strips, 7¾" x 42"; crosscut into 24 squares,
   7¾" x 7¾"

2 strips, 3½" x 42"; crosscut into 20 squares,
   3½" x 3½"

From the dark background fabric, cut:

3 strips, 7¾" x 42"; crosscut into 12 squares,
   7¾" x 7¾"

6 strips, 3½" x 42"; crosscut into 18 rectangles,
   3½" x 9½"; 4 rectangles, 3½" x 6½"; and
   two squares, 3½" x 3½"

6 strips, 4½" x 42"

7 strips, 2½" x 42"

 ## Assembly

Each block is made using the following units:

**2 Medium/Dark
Half-Square-
Triangle Units**   **2 Medium/Light
Half-Square-
Triangle Units**

**4 Corner
Units**   **1 Four-Patch
Unit**

1. To make the half-square-triangle units, mark an X from corner to corner on the wrong side of a 7¾" light square. Layer this square with a 7¾" square of star fabric, right sides together. Sew ¼" on each side of the marked lines. Cut the squares first vertically and then horizontally through the center (3⅞" from the edges). Be careful to make accurate cuts. Cut each piece diagonally on the marked lines and press toward

the darker fabric. Repeat with the remaining star fabrics. You will have a total of 48 units containing medium-dark and light triangles and 48 units containing medium-light and light triangles.

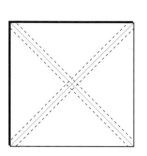 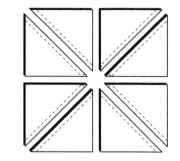

**Dark Star Point
Make 8
of each color.**   **Light Star Point
Make 8
of each color.**

2. To make the corner units, repeat step 1 using the remaining 7¾" light squares and the 7¾" background squares. Make 96 corner units.

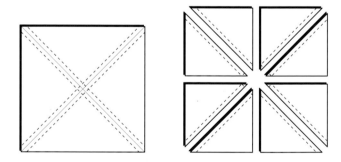

**Corner Unit
Make 96.**

3. Construct a center four-patch unit for each star by sewing two 2" squares of medium-light star fabric to two squares of the corresponding medium-dark star fabric as shown. Press toward the darker fabric. Make four center units from each of the six color groups.

Center Unit
Make 24 total.

4. Arrange two medium-dark star point units, two medium-light star point units, a four-patch unit from the same color group, and four corner units as shown. Be careful to position all the triangles correctly. My most common mistake is to rotate a unit out of position and fail to notice the error until after everything is sewn together! Sew the units into rows, press in opposite directions, and then sew the rows together. Press. I often end up pressing the seams open so that I can see to match the points on the triangles. Make four blocks from each color group.

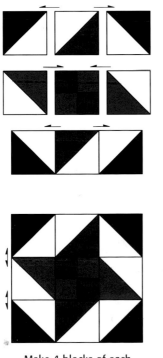

Make 4 blocks of each combination (48 total).

5. Arrange the blocks in six rows of four blocks each. Sew the blocks in each row together. Press seam allowances in the opposite direction from row to row. Sew the rows together and press.

6. Draw a diagonal line from corner to corner on the wrong side of a 3½" light square. Place the square on one end of a 3½" x 9½" background rectangle, right sides together, as shown. Check to be certain the diagonal line is positioned correctly. Sew along the drawn line. Fold a corner of the light square back and compare it to the illustration. Is it sewn to the same end of the rectangle? Is the triangle positioned correctly? If it looks OK, trim the bottom corner of the light fabric, and press the seam as shown on page 68.

Repeat using the remaining 3½" x 9 ½" rectangles and two of the 3½" x 6½" rectangles.

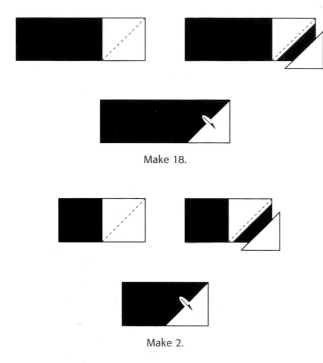

Make 18.

Make 2.

Before piecing the inner border, take time to measure the size of the sewn blocks along the edge of the quilt. Getting the inner border to fit may be tricky if your blocks deviate more than ¼" from a finished size of 9" square. If the blocks are close to 9½" unfinished, the border and quilt top can usually be eased together fairly well. The challenge is to match each light ribbon triangle in the border to the middle row of each block. Here is where you either reap the benefits of "perfect" cutting and sewing, or learn just how far fabric will stretch when "easing to fit"! (Most fabrics will stretch an amazing amount if needed, but batiks are tightly woven and have only a little "give.") If your blocks are odd sizes, and/or you really just want to get the blasted thing finished, forget the pieced inner border and just slap on one or two plain borders as described on pages 15–16. Your quilt will still look lovely. The secret to making a plain border look just as good as a pieced border is to vow never to tell anyone that you considered doing anything other than what you did.

7. To make a pieced side border, sew five of the 9½" border units together, being careful that the triangles face in the correct direction. Add a 6½" border unit to one end and a 3½" background square to the other. Press as shown. Repeat for the other side border. To make the top border, sew four of the 9½" border units together, being careful that the triangles face in the correct direction. Sew a 3½" x 6½" background rectangle to one end and press as shown. Repeat for the bottom border.

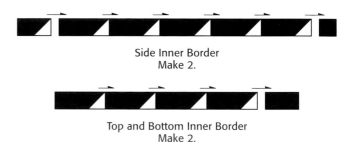

Side Inner Border
Make 2.

Top and Bottom Inner Border
Make 2.

8. Pin the side border units to the quilt top, matching the border triangles with the center rows of the blocks. Sew, easing to fit if necessary. Press toward the border. Pin the top and bottom border units to the quilt top, again matching the triangles with the center row of each block. Sew, easing to fit if necessary. Press toward the border.

9. Sew the 4½" outer-border strips end to end to make one long strip. Measure the length of the quilt top through the center and cut two border strips to this size. Sew a strip to each side of the quilt top. Press toward the outer border.

Measure the width of the quilt top through the center and cut two border strips to this size. Sew to the top and bottom of the quilt top. Press toward the outer border.

10. Layer the pieced backing, batting, and quilt top. Baste the layers together.

11. Quilt as desired.

12. Prepare the binding and sew it to the quilt.

Alternative Fabric Selection

Swap values and create dark ribbons on a light background. Keep the star points and centers medium-light and medium-dark in value. Also, you could make a completely different quilt by using lovely floral prints for the background and ribbons. The pattern will be softened, but it will still be striking if you maintain contrast between the values.

Snail's Trail

Made by Robin Strobel. Quilted by Janice Nelson, 2003.
Finished quilt size: 50" x 58". Finished block size: 8".

Sometimes when I'm halfway through a quilt I think, "There must be a better way." So it was with this classic Snail's Trail. I made my quilt using traditional piecing methods. I cut and cut, and sewed and sewed, and matched points and edges, and ripped out those that somehow slid out of kilter. Then I did it all some more and had only tiny, embryonic snails. Well, such is the way this block is traditionally made— most of the time and effort goes into sewing the little pieces in the center. What troubled me was that my embryonic snails tended to twist and stretch and grow unevenly, and I had a continuous fight to keep the blocks square and the points precise. Making this pattern the "old-fashioned way" requires real precision in cutting and sewing, starting with little tiny pieces in the center and working to the outside! As I was plodding along, I thought of how much easier it would be to paper piece the blocks. I had considered it before I started but decided not to because I had planned on 11¼" finished blocks, and paper-pieced patterns larger than 8" have to be taped together or printed on oversized paper. Well, I ended up making the blocks one round of triangles smaller than I intended (which brought the block size down to 8"). Since I did, I wrote these instructions for you using the paper-piecing method. You may curse me at the beginning, but believe me, by the third round of perfectly pieced points, straight seams, and evenly growing snail embryos, you'll be thanking me.

Successful Fabric Selection

This quilt is probably the easiest project to select fabrics for. You need just two fabrics, one lighter in value than the other. My original intention was to use the same two fabrics in the borders, but when this particular quilt top was finished, I decided I wanted more variety, and so I found three more fabrics: one each for the two borders, and a third for the binding. However, your quilt may look better repeating the block fabrics in the borders. If you buy enough for the borders and then change your mind about using them, you can always use those fabrics on the back.

Materials

Yardage is based on 42"-wide fabric.

2 yards of dark red tone-on-tone print for blocks

2 yards of light print for blocks

⅞ yard of print for outer border

¼ yard of tone-on-tone print for inner border

3⅛ yards for backing (2 widths pieced horizontally)

½ yard for binding

54" x 62" piece of batting

Paper or muslin for foundations

■ Cutting

Note: All strips are cut across the width of the fabric unless indicated otherwise.

From each dark red and light print, cut:

2 strips, 1" x 42"

2 strips, 1¾" x 42"; crosscut each fabric into 30 squares, 1¾" x 1¾". Cut once on the diagonal to make 60 half-square triangles of each fabric.

2 strips, 2" x 42"; crosscut each fabric into 30 squares, 2" x 2". Cut once on the diagonal to make 60 half-square triangles of each fabric.

2 strips, 2½" x 42"; crosscut each fabric into 30 squares, 2½" x 2½". Cut once on the diagonal to make 60 half-square triangles of each fabric.

3 strips, 3" x 42"; crosscut each fabric into 30 squares, 3" x 3". Cut once on the diagonal to make 60 half-square triangles of each fabric.

3 strips, 4" x 42"; crosscut each fabric into 30 squares, 4" x 4". Cut once on the diagonal to make 60 half-square triangles of each fabric.

5 strips, 5¼" x 42"; crosscut each fabric into 30 squares, 5¼" x 5¼". Cut once on the diagonal to make 60 half-square triangles of each fabric.

From the inner-border print, cut:

5 strips, 1¼" x 42"

From the outer-border print, cut:

5 strips, 4½" x 42" (If your fabric has less than 40½" of *usable* width, you will need to cut 6 strips.)

From the binding fabric, cut:

6 strips, 2½" x 42"

■ Assembly

If you have never tried foundation paper piecing, this is a good block to get you started. You have precut your pieces (a little larger than if you were piecing the blocks traditionally), and the shapes are symmetrical, so you don't have to worry about misplacing them in the blocks. A foundation-pieced *block* will end up a mirror image of the foundation *pattern*. If you look at the pattern on page 77, the spirals will appear to spin in the opposite direction as they do in the quilt. You will start by piecing the four-patch center units and placing them in the center of the foundation. Then you will add the triangles, working from the center of the block outward.

1. To make the four-patch center units, sew a 1" red strip to a 1" light print strip along the long edges. Press toward the red. Repeat with the remaining red and light print strips. Cut the strip sets into 60 segments, 1" wide.

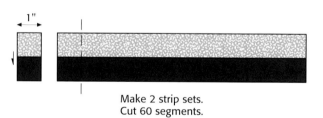

Make 2 strip sets.
Cut 60 segments.

2. Sew two of the segments from step 1 together as shown. Press the seam to one side. Make 30.

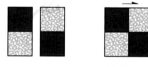

Make 30.

3. Enlarge the pattern 125% that is found on page 77. Every foundation piecer has her own favorite type of foundation. Some people trace the pattern onto lightweight muslin and leave the foundation in the blocks. I like to photocopy the pattern onto the foundation papers that are usually available at my quilt store. They are easy to tear

off the back of the block and the ink does not tend to smear. If I can't find the foundation paper, I use an inexpensive photocopy paper. If using paper (rather than muslin), you will need to trim away the excess paper outside the block. Using your foundation paper or muslin, make 30 copies of the pattern on page 77.

4. With the printed side facing away from you, hold a pattern up to a light and, on the unprinted side, center a four-patch unit, right side up. The seams of the four-patch unit should line up with the lines on the foundation. If you have trouble seeing the lines through the pattern, poke a pin through the dotted line to the unprinted side and use it as a guide. Pin the four-patch unit to the foundation pattern. Note that the four-patch unit is larger than the printed unit.

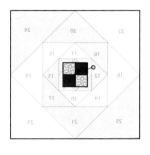

5. Place the long edge of one of the smallest light print triangles, right sides together, on the edge of the four-patch unit that touches triangle 2 of the pattern. Center the tip of the triangle, using the seams of the four-patch unit as a guide, and secure it with a pin. (Place the pin where it won't interfere with the stitching.) It's OK if the triangle does not line up perfectly, because it has been cut slightly oversized.

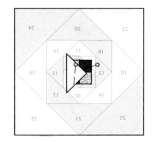

6. Shorten the stitch length on your machine slightly. Turn the foundation over so that the fabric pieces are underneath the paper and stitch directly on the line between the four-patch unit and the triangle. Start and stop a few stitches beyond the line. You don't have to back-stitch. Pull the paper out from the machine and turn it over. Finger-press the triangle toward the outside of the block and check the placement. If you hold the foundation up to the light, the fabric triangle should extend a seam-allowance width past the lines of triangle 2 on the paper and cover part of the shaded triangles near it. The seam allowance does not need to be even, but it does need to have enough fabric to anchor the pieces. If the fabric shifted, and the triangle does not fit, you will have to rip it out and resew it. If you are satisfied with the sewn triangle, trim the "ears" and press. (If you have photo-copied your patterns onto your foundation, use a dry press-cloth on the printed side, because the ink may smear.) You can also trim your seam allowance if it is too untidy.

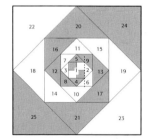 

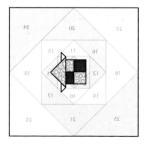

7. Repeat step 5, first with another of the smallest light print triangles, sewing it on the opposite side of the four-patch unit. Then sew two of the smallest red triangles to the remaining two sides of the four-patch unit. You have completed the first "round"!

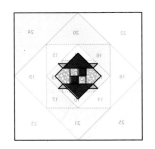

8. Sew the second round like the first, using triangles cut from the 2" squares. Triangles 6 and 7 are the light print, and triangles 8 and 9 are the red print. Continue sewing the triangles to the quilt in order, using the shading on the pattern as a guide to the fabrics. The third round will use triangles cut from 2½" squares, the fourth round will use triangles cut from 3" squares, the fifth round will use triangles cut from 4" squares, and the final round will use triangles cut from 5¼" squares. The dotted lines on the pattern will help you center the tips of the triangles.

9. When all the triangles are sewn to a foundation piece, place the block, paper side up, on your cutting mat. With the ¼" line of your ruler along the edge of the paper, trim to create a perfect ¼" seam allowance.

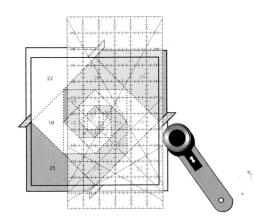

10. Repeat steps 4 through 9 to make 30 Snail's Trail blocks.

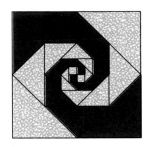

Make 30.

11. Arrange the blocks in six rows of five blocks each. Rotate the blocks so that the fabrics form large, interconnected swirls. Join the blocks into rows, sewing along the edge of the paper but not through it. Press in alternate directions from row to row. Sew the rows together. Press.

74

12. Now comes the messy job of removing all the foundation paper. Work from the outside edge of each block toward its center. I like to slide a prong of a long, thin pair of tweezers under the paper parallel to a seam, and then pull up on the tweezers, letting the stitches rip the paper. If you don't have tweezers, try using the back edge of a seam ripper. Tweezers are also handy for picking out stubborn tufts of paper that can be trapped by the stitching.

13. Sew the 1¼" inner-border strips end to end to make one long strip. Measure the length of the quilt top through the center and cut two border strips to this size. Sew a strip to each side of the quilt top. Press toward the border. Measure the width of the quilt top through the center and cut two border strips to this size. Sew to the top and bottom of the quilt top. Press toward the border.

14. Sew the 4½" outer-border strips end to end to make one long strip. Measure the length of the quilt top through the center and cut two border strips to this size. Sew a strip to each side of the quilt top. Press toward the outer border. Measure the width of the quilt top through the center and cut two border strips to this size. Sew to the top and bottom of the quilt top. Press toward the outer border.

15. Layer the pieced backing, batting, and quilt top. Baste the layers together.

16. Quilt as desired.

17. Prepare the binding and sew it to the quilt.

▨ Alternative Fabric Selection

You might draw inspiration from one of this block's other names: Ocean Waves. Make a quilt in colors of the sea using batik fabrics. Many batiks exhibit wonderful shifts of color across the fabric, and a quilt made with such a fabric will have a lovely richness and depth. Open up the fabrics to get a good look at the entire range of colors and value before you purchase them. Be careful that the shifts in color and value don't make it difficult to tell which fabric is the light and which is the dark, especially since they will be cut into very small pieces.

This pattern also makes a great quilt made from scraps. Divide your fabrics into lights and darks; then randomly cut the pieces.

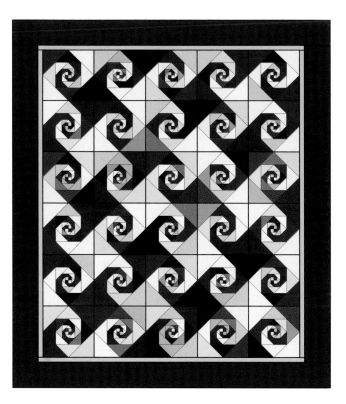

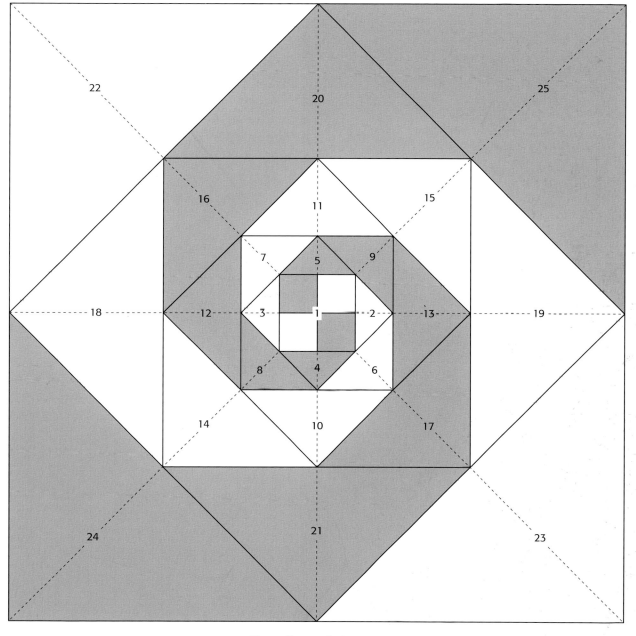

Snail's Trail Foundation Pattern
Enlarge pattern 125%.
Make 30 copies.

Double Star

Made by Robin Strobel. Quilted by Pam Clarke, 2003.
Finished quilt size: 77" x 89½". Finished block size: 12½".

Two different stars sparkle across this quilt. Thin blue stars are the focus of the block. Rose sawtooth stars and dark "lattice" form the secondary pattern when the blocks are joined. I wanted the design to be dramatic, so I chose high-contrast light and dark fabrics. However, since I didn't want the overall effect to look too harsh, I tried to soften the design with two lovely floral prints.

 ## Successful Fabric Selection

Keep the background fabric distinctly light in comparison to the other three fabrics you choose. I wanted a dark print for the lattice design in order to increase the contrast with the background, and I left the middle value range for the stars. If you stick with primarily neutral colors for the background and dark prints, I think the stars would be effective in just about any color. I found a lovely, clear blue for the thin stars and a rose print that worked well with the main floral. There are two different black floral prints in this quilt—a smaller-scale print in the blocks and a larger companion print for the outer border and binding. Don't worry if you can't find two matching florals. Just combine the yardages and make the blocks, outer border, and binding out of the same fabric.

Materials

Yardage is based on 42"-wide fabric.

2¼ yards of large-scale black floral print for outer border and binding

2¼ yards of tan background print for blocks

2 yards of medium-scale black floral print for blocks

1½ yards of blue print for blocks and inner border

1¼ yards of rose print for blocks

5½ yards for backing (2 lengths pieced vertically)

81" x 94" piece of batting

Template plastic

Cutting

Note: All strips are cut across the width of the fabric unless indicated otherwise.

From the tan background print, cut:
6 strips, 5½" x 42"
5 strips, 6¾" x 42"; crosscut into 30 squares, 6¾" x 6¾" (If your fabric has less than 40½" of *usable* width, you will need to cut 6 strips.)

From the blue print, cut:
6 strips, 5½" x 42"
7 strips, 2" x 42"

From the rose print, cut:
5 strips, 6¾" x 42"; crosscut into 30 squares, 6¾" x 6¾" (If your fabric has less than 40½" of *usable* width, you will need to cut 6 strips.)

From the medium-scale black floral print, cut:
21 strips, 3" x 42"; crosscut into 270 squares, 3" x 3"

From the large-scale black floral print, cut:
8 strips, 6" x 42"
9 strips, 2½" x 42"

Assembly

Each block is made using the following units:

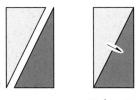

9 Squares | 8 Half-Square-Triangle Units | 4 Half-Rectangle Units

1. Make a template using the pattern on page 83. Cut 120 triangles each from the 5½" tan and 5½" blue strips. Refer to page 11 in "Quilting Basics." Be careful to always cut the triangles with both the fabric and the templates facing right side up. To make the thin star points, sew the tan triangles to the blue triangles as shown. These edges are cut on the bias, so be careful not to stretch them out of shape when sewing. Press toward the blue triangles. Make 120 half-rectangle units.

Make 120.

2. To make the half-square-triangle units, mark an X from corner to corner on the wrong side of a tan square. Layer this square with a rose print square, right sides together. Sew ¼" on each side of the marked lines. Cut the squares first vertically and then horizontally through the center (3⅜" from the edges). Be careful to make accurate cuts. Cut each piece diagonally on the marked lines and press toward the rose fabric.

Repeat with the remaining tan squares and rose squares to make a total of 240 half-square-triangle units.

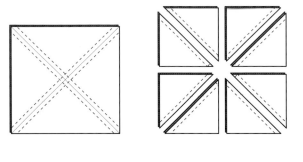

Make 240.

3. Arrange two half-square-triangle units from step 2 with two 3" black floral squares as shown. Be careful to arrange the half-square-triangle units so that the rose print meets at the center. Sew each black square to a half-square-triangle unit. Press toward the black. Sew the two units together to make a corner unit and press. Repeat to make 120 corner units.

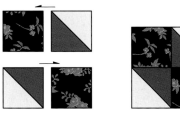

Corner Unit
Make 120.

4. Arrange four half-rectangle units, four corner units, and one 3" black floral square as shown. Sew the units into rows and press as shown. Sew the rows together. If you have trouble matching

the points, you may find the section "Quilting Basics" on page 7 helpful. Press. Make 30 blocks.

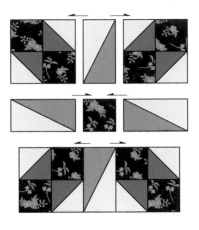

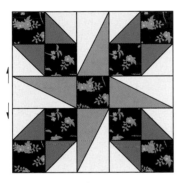

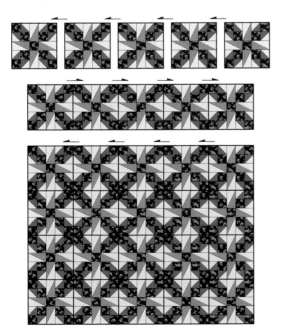

Make 30.

5. Arrange the blocks in six rows of five blocks each. Stitch the blocks into rows and press in alternate directions from row to row. Stitch the rows together and press.

6. Sew the 2" blue inner-border strips end to end to make one long strip. Measure the length of the quilt top through the center and cut two border strips to this size. Sew a strip to each side of the quilt top. Press toward the border. Measure the width of the quilt top through the center and cut two border strips to this size. Sew to the top and bottom of the quilt top. Press toward the border.

7. Sew the 6" black outer-border strips end to end to make one long strip. Measure the length of the quilt top through the center and cut two border strips to this size. Sew a strip to each side of the quilt top. Press toward the outer border. Measure the width of the quilt top through the center and cut two border strips to this size. Sew to the top and bottom of the quilt top. Press toward the outer border.

8. Layer the pieced backing, batting, and quilt top. Baste the layers together.

9. Quilt as desired.

10. Prepare the binding and sew it to the quilt.

81

Alternative Fabric Selection

Shifting the light and dark values will give an entirely different look to this pattern. In the first example, I made the background very dark, the lattice medium, and the thin star points very light.

In the second example, the sawtooth stars are a bright white, the thin stars a dark red, the background a medium green, and the lattice a dark green.

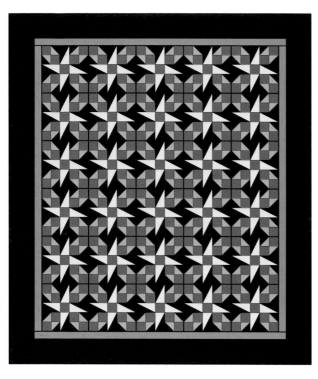

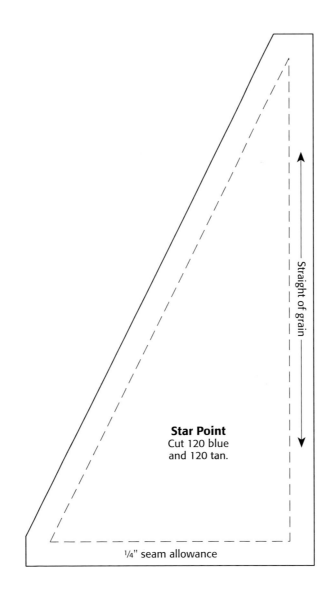

Star Point
Cut 120 blue
and 120 tan.

Straight of grain

¼" seam allowance

Laurel's Stars

Made by Laurel Strand. Quilted by Pam Clarke, 2003.
Finished quilt size: 44" x 51½". Finished block size: 7½".

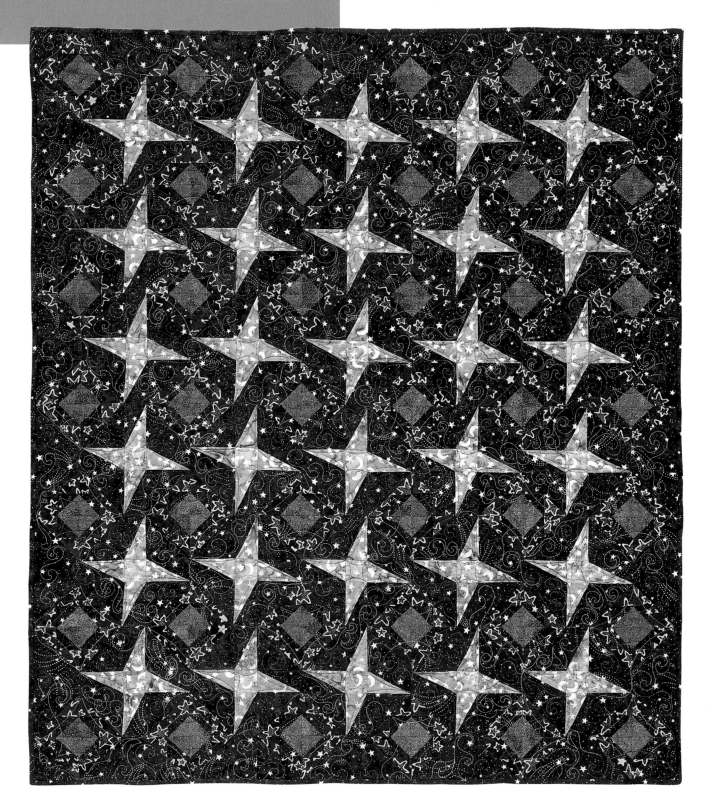

Laurel is a very talented illustrator at Martingale & Company who brings
a fine sense of color and design (and perfectionism) to her quiltmaking. The thin
blue stars in this quilt are nicely complemented by the secondary square-in-a-square
pattern that emerges. This block is easier than it looks, because it features a
quick-piecing technique found in the book *Triangle Tricks*,
published in 2003 by Martingale & Company.

Successful Fabric Selection

Start with a light-value fabric for the stars and a nice dark fabric for the background. These are the most noticeable fabrics in the quilt, so they should complement each other as well as create good contrast. Choose two medium-value prints (or one medium and one medium-light value) for the corners of the blocks. You will want these fabrics to contrast with the dark background as well, so consider how 1½" pieces of the fabrics will look. Laurel wanted the blue stars to really sparkle over the surface of the quilt, so she chose fairly dark fabrics for the corners, but notice they still look distinctly different from the background.

Materials

Yardage is based on 42"-wide fabric.

2⅜ yards of dark blue background fabric for blocks, pieced border, and binding

⅞ yard of medium-value pink star print for blocks

⅝ yard of light blue print for blocks

½ yard of medium-value purple dot print for blocks

2¾ yards for backing (2 widths pieced horizontally)

48" x 56" piece of batting

Template plastic

Cutting

Note: All strips are cut across the width of the fabric unless indicated otherwise.

From the dark blue background fabric, cut:
4 strips, 3½" x 42"
3 strips, 4¾" x 42"; crosscut into 21 squares, 4¾" x 4¾"
8 strips, 4½" x 42"; crosscut into 84 rectangles, 3½" x 4½"
2 strips, 2" x 42"; crosscut into 22 rectangles, 2" x 3½"
5 strips, 2½" x 42"

From the light blue print, cut:
4 strips, 3½" x 42"
2 strips, 2" x 42"; crosscut into 30 squares, 2" x 2"

From the purple dot print, cut:
3 strips, 4¾" x 42"; crosscut into 21 squares, 4¾" x 4¾"

From the pink star print, cut:
9 strips, 3" x 42"; crosscut into 168 rectangles, 2" x 3"

 Assembly

Each block is made using the following units:

4 Corner Units   4 Half-Rectangle Units   1 Square

1. Make a template using the pattern on page 89. Cut 120 triangles each from the 3½" dark blue background the 3½" light blue strips. Be careful to always cut the triangles with both the fabric and the template facing right side up. (See page 11 in "Quilting Basics.") To make the star points, sew a dark blue triangle to a light blue triangle as shown. These edges are cut on the bias, so be careful not to stretch them out of shape. Press toward the dark blue. Repeat with the remaining dark blue and light blue triangles to make 120 half-rectangle units.

Make 120.

2. To make the small half-square-triangle units for the block corners, mark an X from corner to corner on the wrong side of a purple dot square. Layer this square with a dark blue square, right sides together. Sew ¼" on each side of the marked lines. Cut the squares first vertically and then horizontally through the center (2⅜" from the edges). Be careful to make accurate cuts. Cut each piece diagonally on the marked lines. Press toward the dark blue. Repeat with the remaining 4¾" squares to make 168 half-square-triangle units.

Make 168.

3. Sew each triangle unit made in step 2 to one end of a pink rectangle, being careful to position the units as shown. (It is very easy to rotate the triangle units incorrectly, so double-check yourself before sewing!) Press toward the pink rectangles.

Make 168.

4. Sew together two of the units made in step 3 as shown. Clip the fabric at the center, just up to the seam but not through it. Press the two sides in opposite directions as shown. (Keep going, this really works!) Repeat with the remaining units.

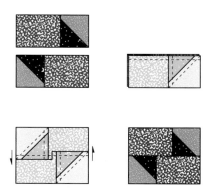

5. Turn one of the units made in step 4 wrong side up. Place the 45° line of your ruler along the right edge of the unit so that the ruler's edge intersects the corner seams of the lower half-square-triangle unit as shown. This will be a stitching line, so mark it with a pencil that will show up against the fabric. (To ensure that the mark will not bleed through to the front, I usually use either a regular or a white pencil.)

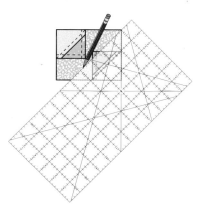

86

6. Mark a second stitching line on the same unit by placing the 45° line of the ruler along the bottom edge of the unit, with the ruler's edge intersecting the corner seams of the upper half-square-triangle unit as shown.

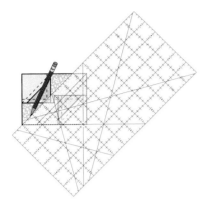

7. Layer the unit from step 6 with a 3½" x 4½" dark blue rectangle, right sides together. Pin and sew along the marked lines. Cut between the sewn lines. Press each piece toward the large blue triangle. Repeat steps 5–7 with all the units made in step 4 and the remaining blue rectangles. You will have 168 corner units. (This unit is sometimes called a "shaded four-patch" and may be used on its own as a block or, as in this quilt, as a unit within a block. The book *Triangle Tricks*, from which I learned this technique, has some great examples of shaded four-patch quilts and includes instructions for making these blocks in sizes from 2" to 12".)

Corner Unit
Make 168.

8. Arrange four half-rectangle units, four corner units, and a 2" light blue square as shown. Stitch into rows. Press. Stitch the rows together and press. Make 30 blocks.

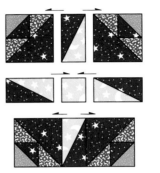 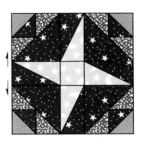

Center Block
Make 30.

9. Arrange the blocks in six rows of five blocks each. Sew the blocks together into rows, and press in alternate directions from row to row. Sew the rows together. Press.

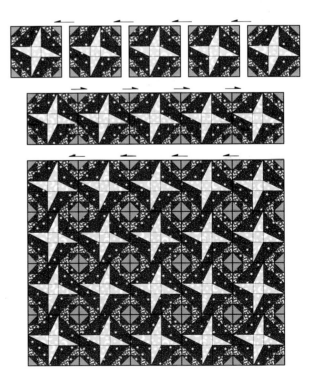

10. To make the borders, arrange two corner units from step 7 with a 2" x 3½" dark blue rectangle as shown. Sew together and press toward the dark blue rectangle. Make 22 border blocks.

Border Block
Make 22.

11. For the side border units, sew six border blocks together as shown. Press as needed to accommodate block seams in the quilt. Make two.

12. For the top and bottom borders, sew five border blocks together. Add a corner unit from step 7 to each end, being careful to position the corner blocks as shown. Press as needed to accommodate block seams in the quilt. Make two.

Side Border
Make 2.

Top and Bottom Border
Make 2.

13. Sew the side border units to the quilt center. Press. Sew the top and bottom border units to the quilt center. Press.

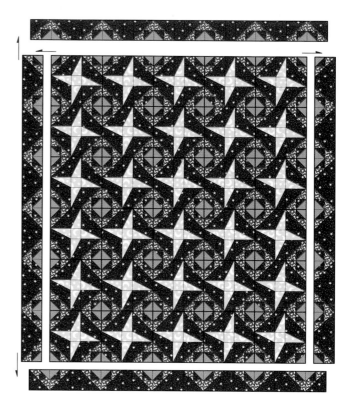

14. Layer the pieced backing, batting, and quilt top. Baste the layers together.

15. Quilt as desired.

16. Prepare the binding and sew it to the quilt.

■ Alternative Fabric Selection

Make yourself a quilt for the holidays with red stars against a white background. Use a medium green and a light green for the corner triangles.

You can also make a quilt with a bold, masculine feel by choosing black, white, and red fabrics. Note that I changed the color of the center of the stars.

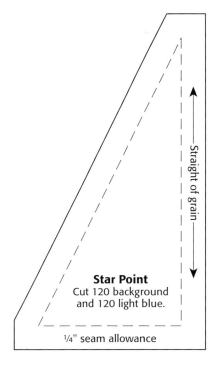

Star Point
Cut 120 background
and 120 light blue.

Straight of grain

¼" seam allowance

Terry's Cherries

Made by Terry Martin. Quilted by Pam Clarke, 2003.
Finished quilt size: 69" x 69". Finished block size: 10½".

Terry, one of my coworkers, is a talented quilt designer and author. She excels at using those wonderful novelty prints that we love to purchase but often leave in our stashes because we have trouble incorporating them into a quilt. She found this traditional block, Lacy Lattice Work, in Barbara Brackman's *Encyclopedia of Pieced Quilt Patterns.* (See "Resources" on page 96.) When Terry and I talked about using a cherry print as the featured fabric, she brought in those from her stash—an entire tub's worth! It was like having my own "personal quilting shopper" at work! The block is not difficult to piece and there are few seams to match, but it does require an extra step when sewing the center square.

Successful Fabric Selection

Almost any four fabrics that look pleasing together and create clear contrast will work well in this design. Choose a dark print for the background and a contrasting fabric for the long rectangles. A strong contrast will make the rectangles appear to spin against the background. Two more prints that contrast with the background are used for the corner triangles. The four fabrics in Terry's quilt could have been switched around in different positions, and the results, while different, would still create an effective, dynamic pattern.

Materials

Yardage is based on 42"-wide fabric.

3⅝ yards of cherry print for blocks, border, and binding

1¼ yards of red tone-on-tone print for blocks

¾ yard of gold tone-on-tone print for blocks

¾ yard of green tone-on-tone print for blocks

4¼ yards for backing (2 widths pieced either horizontally or vertically)

73" x 73" piece of batting

Template plastic

Cutting

Note: All strips are cut across the width of the fabric unless indicated otherwise.

From the cherry print, cut:

5 strips, 6 ½" x 42"

2 strips, 16⅛" x 42"; crosscut into 3 squares, 16⅛" x 16⅛". Cut twice diagonally to yield 12 side setting triangles. From the remainder of the strips, cut 2 squares, 8⅜" x 8⅜". Cut once diagonally to yield 4 corner setting triangles.

7 strips, 5" x 42"

8 strips, 2½" x 42"

From the gold tone-on-tone print, cut:

3 strips, 6½" x 42"

2 strips, 2" x 42"; crosscut into 25 squares, 2" x 2"

From the green tone-on-tone print, cut:

3 strips, 6½" x 42"

From the red tone-on-tone print, cut:

5 strips, 6½" x 42"; crosscut into 100 rectangles, 2" x 6½"

Assembly

Each block is made using the following units:

| 2 Green Half-Rectangle Units | 2 Gold Half-Rectangle Units | 4 Red Rectangles | 1 Gold Square |

1. With right sides up, cut the 6½" cherry print strips into 100 triangles, using the template provided on page 95. I like to layer several strips together, right sides facing up, and cut several triangles at the same time. With right sides up, cut the 6½" gold strips and green strips into 56 triangles each. Be careful to always cut the triangles with both the fabric and the template facing right side up. Refer to "Quilting Basics" on page 7.

2. Sew 50 cherry print triangles to the green triangles and the remaining 50 cherry print triangles to the gold triangles. Press toward the cherry print. You will have six green and six gold triangles left over. Set these aside.

Make 50.

Make 50.

3. Sew a red rectangle to the cherry print on each half-rectangle unit made in step 2. Press toward

the red. You will have 50 units with green triangles and 50 units with gold triangles.

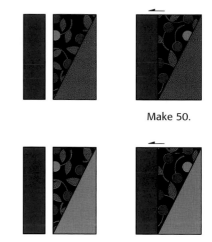

Make 50.

Make 50.

4. Arrange one gold square, two green triangle units, and two gold triangle units into a block. The green triangles and gold triangles should be on the outer corners of the block as shown.

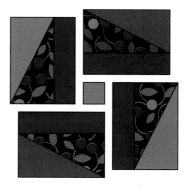

5. With right sides together, align one edge of the gold square with a red rectangle as shown. Beginning at the midpoint of the square's edge, backstitch just one or two stitches and then sew half of the square to the edge of the rectangle with a partial seam. Finger-press toward the red rectangle.

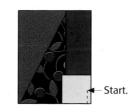 

←Start.

92

6. Sew the unit from step 5 to the red rectangle from the lower neighboring unit. Press toward the red rectangle. Continuing around the block, sew the units together in the same manner. When you sew the final seam, you will be completing the partial seam created in step 5. Take a few stitches on top of the previous stitches and continue sewing to the end. Press. Repeat steps 4–6 to make 25 blocks.

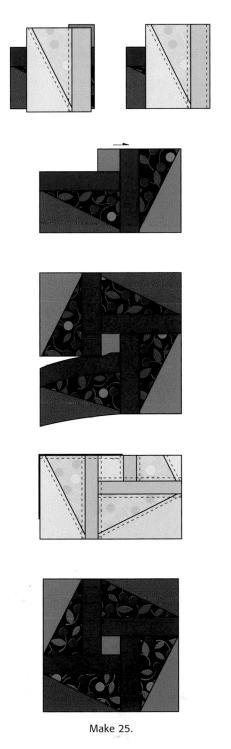

Make 25.

7. The technique I use to sew the gold and green triangles to the side setting triangles is a little unorthodox, but it is quick and I find it easier than the usual methods. First, press under a ¼" seam allowance along the long edge of each of the remaining six green and six gold triangles. (Because these points do not have to match up with a seam, you can "guesstimate" the quarter inch.) Lay one of these triangles on a cherry print side setting triangle, right sides up, with the 90° corners and two edges matching.

8. Slide a pin under the small triangle's short edge, poking through the pressed seam allowance and the large triangle. Repeat at the other end of the small triangle. Carefully flip the small triangle open, being careful not to shift the pressed seam against the large triangle. Pin completely in place and stitch along the fold line. Flip back to the corner, press, and check to be sure the small triangle has not shifted too far out of place. ("Too far" translates to more than can be covered within the seam allowance.) You can trim the excess cherry fabric under the small triangle, or do as I did and leave the double layer of fabric. (This has the advantage of providing the edge of the side setting triangle to align with the blocks.) Make six side setting triangles with

93

green corners and six side setting triangles with gold corners.

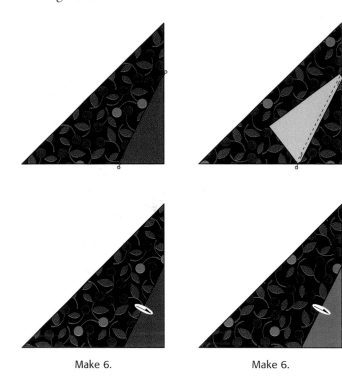

Make 6.   Make 6.

9. Arrange the blocks and the side setting triangles into rows as shown above right. Stitch the blocks into rows and press the rows in alternate directions. Sew the rows together and press. Sew the four cherry print corner setting triangles to the quilt. Press toward the corners.

10. Sew the 5" border strips together end to end to make one long strip. Measure the length of the quilt top through the center. Cut two border strips to this size and sew to the sides of the quilt top, matching the centers and easing as needed. Press toward the border. Measure the width of the quilt top through the center. Cut two border strips to this size and sew to the top and bottom of the quilt top, matching the centers and easing as needed. Press toward the border.

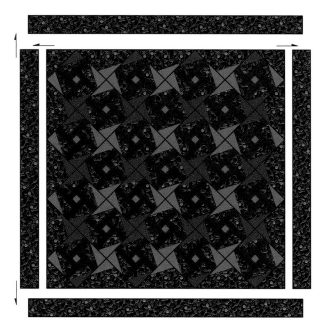

11. Layer the pieced backing, batting, and quilt top. Baste the layers together.

12. Quilt as desired.

13. Prepare the binding and sew it to the quilt.

Alternative Fabric Selection

You can use just three fabrics and make a wonderful quilt that will feature a favorite print. Instead of using two different fabrics to make the corner triangles, place your favorite print in those positions (simply combine the gold and green yardages). Choose a bright fabric for the red rectangles and a subtle background instead of the cherry print.

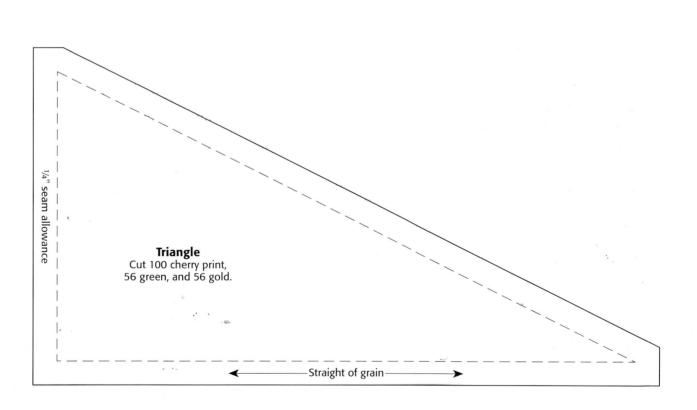

¼" seam allowance

Triangle
Cut 100 cherry print,
56 green, and 56 gold.

◄——————— Straight of grain ———————►

Resources

Loving Stitches: A Guide to Fine Hand Quilting, Revised Edition by Jeana Kimball, 2003, Martingale & Company, ISBN 1-56477-498-8

Hand-quilting instruction

Encyclopedia of Pieced Quilt Patterns by Barbara Brackman, 1993, American Quilter's Society, ISBN 0-89145-815-8

The most complete resource of traditional quilt blocks

Machine Quilting Made Easy! by Maurine Noble, 1994, Martingale & Company, ISBN 1-56477-074-5

Machine-quilting instruction

Heirloom Machine Quilting by Harriet Hargrave, 1995, C & T Publishing, ISBN 0-91488-192-2

Machine-quilting instruction

Triangle Tricks: One Easy Unit, Dozens of Gorgeous Quilts, 2003, Martingale & Company, ISBN 1-56477-467-8

Quick and accurate technique for creating shaded four-patch blocks

About the Author

Robin Strobel enjoys living in the Pacific Northwest, where there are no fewer than 14 quilt stores reachable in an hour or less from her home. She has been quilting for more than 15 years and is the author of *The Casual Quilter,* published by Martingale & Company. Although she has degrees in both biology and education, she has found her niche as a teacher of quilting classes and an illustrator for quilting and knitting books.